The

HEALING
HOME

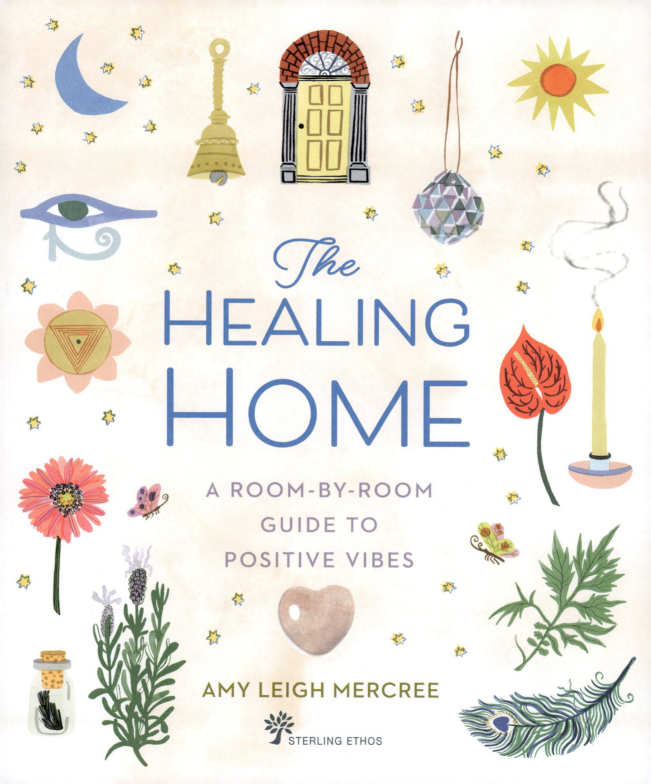

The
HEALING
HOME

A ROOM-BY-ROOM
GUIDE TO
POSITIVE VIBES

AMY LEIGH MERCREE

STERLING ETHOS

STERLING ETHOS
New York

An Imprint of Sterling Publishing Co., Inc.

ISBN 978-1-4549-4483-6
ISBN 978-1-4549-4614-4 (e-book)

Distributed in Canada by Sterling Publishing Co., Inc.
c/o Canadian Manda Group, 664 Annette Street
Toronto, Ontario M6S 2C8, Canada
Distributed in the United Kingdom by GMC Distribution Services
Castle Place, 166 High Street, Lewes, East Sussex BN7 1XU, England
Distributed in Australia by NewSouth Books
University of New South Wales, Sydney, NSW 2052, Australia

For information about custom editions, special sales, and premium and corporate purchases, please contact Sterling Special Sales at specialsales@sterlingpublishing.com.

Manufactured in Malaysia

2 4 6 8 10 9 7 5 3 1

sterlingpublishing.com

Cover design, endpapers, and interior by Gina Bonanano
Illustrations by Nina Chakrabarti unless otherwise noted on page 183

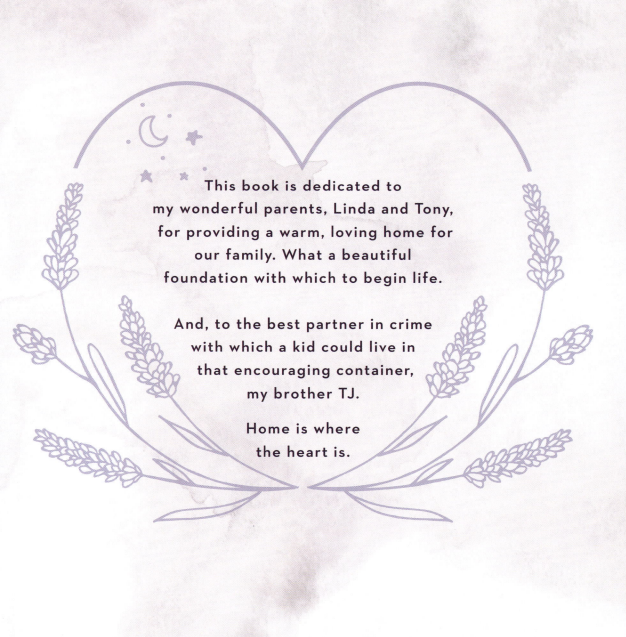

This book is dedicated to
my wonderful parents, Linda and Tony,
for providing a warm, loving home for
our family. What a beautiful
foundation with which to begin life.

And, to the best partner in crime
with which a kid could live in
that encouraging container,
my brother TJ.

Home is where
the heart is.

CNTENTS

Note from Amy

$\mathcal{M}$y name is Amy Leigh Mercree, and I have been a medical intuitive for over twenty years. It has been my privilege and joy to work with my clients and learn how the body works on subtle energetic levels. They have taught me that we can manifest health in endless ways. Over all these years, one thing that I have come to understand is the way that our dwellings affect every facet of our being: we spend most of our time in our home, so it has a profound effect on our bodies, our minds, and our spirits. And even before the pandemic, when we all spent so much time at home, we would sleep there, eat there, play there, and create there. Many of us also began to work from our homes instead of going into an office.

My job is to advise people on how to set up their homes in a way that energetically, physically, emotionally, mentally, and spiritually supports their way of life. Specifically, I want to see my clients living in a home that helps them obtain their hearts' desires. We all have states of being to which we aspire. Even though we may know intellectually that being present and mindful is a good thing, intuitively it can be challenging to balance that peacefulness with all of our future goals, dreams, and ambitions. We have experiences that we desire: a summer trip to Europe, a promotion, ten thousand new social media followers. As humans, we are conditioned to look to the future. That may be one of the reasons that we evolve—because we are wired to strive for more. So, in this book, I want to help you set up your living space as a peaceful nest to help you enjoy every moment of your life with mindful presence while also providing a place full of energy that helps you manifest your desires.

Yes, making that kind of home can seem like a big task! But our homes can be places where we can be present and grateful and appreciate our lives but also get excited about the process of making them better.

A big part of what I want you take away from this book are the following truths:

1. Everything is alive.
2. Everything is connected.
3. Everything is energy.

Using these simple yet powerful truths, we will unlock the power of your space and magnetize your desires so that they bring you health and joy.

In this book, I have laid out ways to apply contemporary and ancient knowledge from all over the world to the arrangement of our homes. We will draw insight from aromatherapy practices, botanical healing, and the contemporary use of minerals and crystals as well as Taoist and Vedic philosophy, Buddhist tradition, Native American ritual and mythology, and so much more.

Let's take this journey together! Let's overhaul the energy of your living space, no matter how small or big, and align your home, your health, and your life. Take the teachings in this book and apply them to your home to create the life experience you desire. I'm honored and excited to be your guide. So, with fresh eyes, open the front door and step inside with me—let's create the healing home you've always dreamed of!

XO,

Amy

How to Use This Book

I created *The Healing Home* because I want you to have the life of your dreams. I know that the way you arrange your home infuses it with energy, which is key if you want to have the momentum necessary to accomplish what you want to achieve. When I speak to clients who want to make changes so they can reach their goals, I ask them to take stock of their lives and tell me what isn't working—what frustrates them. We often discover that there are so many facets of their existence that could flow more easily if they had systems to support their daily activities. For example, if you value order, a simple habit of making your bed upon rising can bring a sense of routine that feels comforting and grounding to some. On the other hand, if too much structure feels suffocating, then you might choose to keep your evenings unscheduled and spontaneous to balance your more traditionally scheduled workdays. That is why *The Healing Home* is broken into rooms: each room is a place where you perform certain tasks or activities over and over again, so if we look at those activities with open eyes, we can figure out how to make them easier and more natural. This process is meant to be easy, and the ideal result is also ease.

The goal is to make you feel happy as well as harmonious in your relationships and your living space, physically healthy and spiritually whole. You should be able to embrace the energy in your own body, your magnetic charisma, and your own beautiful radiance. When you feel like you have a holistic understanding of the way in which you interact with your home, you will feel more empowered to take the helm and own your life with sovereignty, confidence, and authority. You will gain an understanding of the way in which you live your life so that you can improve it from the moment you wake up to the last second before you go to sleep. So think of this book as an essential guide to that process, whether you do it all at once or over time.

Although this book is organized room by room, the sequence is up to you. You can start anywhere you like! If you feel like you want to make over a particular room, you can simply start there, or you can go through the whole house beginning at the front door where this book begins. Each section includes in-depth energetic makeovers, but I have also included quick fixes that can produce results right away. The introduction will cover some of the main schools of thought and healing traditions that we will lean on in reconsidering your space, such as feng shui and Taoism, shamanic techniques including using sound to clear dense energy from a room, and utilizing certain plants to bring specific types of energy to areas of the home. The approach to each room will be primarily based on its energy, but that will also mean addressing the other physical, mental, and spiritual ways we interact with the space—so that could be how it smells, the beauty and clarity of its light, its organization, its ability to support growing things such as houseplants, and more. We will apply these modalities to healing the energy in multiple rooms, so you can read about their basic tenets in the introductory material before you dive in to specific exercises. And, if you'd like to get to the exercises right away, that's also fine! Go ahead and skip to the room you'd like to work on, because the exercises in that section will refer back to the introduction in case you'd like to learn more.

Everything is alive and interconnected. We will harness that truth and power and align your home to your dreams, wants, and needs with grace and ease. Let's jump in and create your healing home!

EVERYTHING IS ENERGY

There are a number of faith traditions that are based on the concept that everything is energy: physical objects, people, animals, and plants. For example, Taoism teaches that everything is comprised of energy called *chi*, which is always seeking harmony and alignment. Taoist philosophy is the origin of feng shui and Traditional Chinese Medicine, which includes acupuncture, acupressure, cupping, and much more. When we work with Taoist philosophy in the home, we find ourselves looking for ways to align the energy of our bodies with the spaces in which we move. This leads us to the use of the *bagua*, a chart specifying the energetic areas of the home. *Bagua* means "eight areas" in Chinese, and accordingly, this chart is divided into sections in which specific kinds of energy are supported. In each chapter, we will look at the bagua according to its impact upon that area of the home. We will use the bagua to place what we call cures in key places in the home to optimize its energy.

Everything Is Connected

Vastu means "dwelling" in Hindu. This ancient architectural system was derived from the Vedas, sacred Hindu texts dating back to 1500 BCE. In the past, Vastu was used to plan cities. Its rules could be scaled up or down and were just as effective for mapping a metropolis as they were for individual dwellings, large or small. We will use the theories of Vastu to develop the creative energy of your home. We will also be delving into the way that Vedic and Buddhist philosophy can influence our spaces in each area of our lives and the corresponding rooms of our homes. For example, the chakra system can give us insight into our bodies, and our ability to meditate and use mindfulness within the home can anchor the energies we desire. We'll dive deep into that with lots of fun and practical exercises and rituals. The universe is an interconnected web, and we will cover the many philosophies, traditions, and systems that support that concept.

Everything Is Alive

I have taught cross-cultural shamanism for over twenty years. Shamanism is the discipline, art, and science of journeying into other dimensions. By reaching into those alternate realities, practitioners can heal themselves or others or gain valuable information. In layperson's terms, shamanism is how to talk to spirit guides.

I apprenticed for over a decade with my medicine teacher, Laurie. She crossed to the other side of the veil in 2019. She had participated in an oral tradition of memory keeping that went back several generations. Because of my teacher, and her teacher, and her teacher's teacher, and so on, I can help you understand how to retrieve energy from the next world and bring it back to this one for greater wholeness. By using shamanic techniques, you can also work toward extracting negative energy from your home. I'll teach you how to do that as well as connect with useful spirit energies through ceremony, ritual, and even physical exercises. We also can bring in the help of our benevolent ancestors to infuse our space with support.

By working in certain areas of your home, you will be able to move and change the energy. Many of the healing traditions in our world are the result of a connection to the universal current that flows through everything. We are going to explore other methods of working with energy, because it is so valuable in understanding and improving our relationship with our spaces. You will see elements of various methods of energy work sprinkled throughout this book. Some of those techniques include plants, herbs, crystals, and essential oils.

We'll also discuss the way that we can use and move these energies to create the environment we desire in our homes. Setting an intention for your spaces' purpose is also crucial. I'll guide you through manifesting your dreams in your home.

Note: This book is intended for insight, education, and informational purposes only. I am not a licensed medical doctor, chiropractor, osteopathic physician, naturopathic doctor, nutritionist, pharmacist, psychologist, psychotherapist, or other formally licensed healthcare professional. Therefore, I do not render medical, psychological, or other professional advice or treatment, nor do I provide or prescribe any medical diagnosis, treatment, medication, or remedy. Nothing in this book should be construed to constitute healthcare advice or medical diagnosis, treatment, or prescribing. Information or guidance provided by me should not be construed as a promise of benefits, a claim of cures, or a guarantee of results to be achieved. I make no guarantees or warranties related to this book.

Our Healing Home Practice

In each room, you will find a series of touchpoints on which you may place your focus. You can choose to use as many of them as you'd like—just the one you like the most, or an entire chapter's worth. You may come back to my recommendations after you have tried out a few and experienced their results. Each chapter begins with healing-power mantras, so I encourage you to start by saying these mantras aloud. Then try speaking them as you apply the other remedies to infuse them with even more power.

In each chapter, you will find hints and tips using aromatherapy, plants, crystals, spirit guides, and ancestral energy as well as clearings, rituals, and ceremonies. We will explore yin and yang energy in each space and Taoist hints and tips from feng shui. We'll also weave in Vedic and other elemental healing including chakras, and we will do a quick holistic health check at the end.

Aromatherapy

Evocative scent is a huge part of feeling at ease with your space. Essential oils not only have amazing health effects, but they also smell great! And their energetic properties can make you feel calm, energized, passionate, or a whole

variety of other qualities depending upon what mood you want to set in a particular room.

Always use only pure organic essential oils and avoid synthetic fragrances. When shopping for oils, watch out for phrases such as *fragrance oil*, *nature identical oil*, and *perfume oil*. None of these indicate a pure essential oil, and some even have added chemicals. Organic essential oils are grown without herbicides and pesticides. Because plants *do* absorb these substances, it follows that we will absorb these chemicals into our systems when we use them—so avoid anything that isn't organic, if you can.

Some companies market their essential oils with terms such as *therapeutic grade,* *food grade*, *aromatherapy grade*, *medicinal grade*, or label them *certified*. But there is no formally approved grading standard system in the essential oil industry.

If you're looking at a product from a reputable company, then you are more likely to be able to trust that company's grading system to be genuine—but always do your research. Also, check if the company's products are gas chromatography and mass spectrometry tested, and make sure they are not in plastic bottles, but in dark-colored glass bottles, which prevent the oils from degrading when exposed to light. Stay away from cheaper oils—opting for quality is well worth it in this case!

In labeling an essential oil as a *therapeutic-grade oil*, companies mean that:

* It's distilled without using chemicals.
* It's more expensive to produce because it requires hundreds of pounds of plant material to distill only a single pound of oil.

So even though the term *therapeutic grade* isn't certified by any particular grading system, it is an indication of quality that is worth looking for.

Scenting the Home with Essential Oils

Diffusion is the simplest, most common method of applying aromatics to your home. Essential oil diffusers are versatile and easy to use. Cold-air diffusers use ultrasonic vibrations that break the tiny oil particles into a mist that remains suspended in the air for hours. Their aroma  fills the atmosphere and breathing them in has specific physical and emotional benefits. Humidifiers, vaporizers, vents, or fans are all good alternatives if you don't have a diffuser around.

If you want to get started without buying any special equipment, you can boil a pot of water on the stove and then add the oils you desire. As the water boils, the scent from the oils will fill the air. Alternatively, you can pour water and a few drops of your essential oil in a *microwave-safe* bowl and heat until boiling. For safety reasons, if you use the stove or microwave, make sure the water does not completely evaporate.

Plants

Houseplants are a delightful way to bring living chi into a room! It is important they are kept well tended, clean, well watered, and in excellent condition. An ill or wilting houseplant equals poor chi. Living plants are ideal, but if they aren't a practical option for you, there are beautiful artificial options that will have a similar effect. But remember, even artificial plants must be regularly dusted and should be discarded when not looking perfectly pristine.

Flowers are also a great option. They bring light and life to any room. Flower petals are the living essence of a blooming plant and are designed by nature to be beautiful to entice insects to pollinate. Blooms are an expression of beauty and life, and they can bring energy and life into your home. I'll recommend some houseplants and flowers for each room to help enliven its moving chi.

Crystals

Crystals are beautiful conduits for energy. They are living beings and are to be respected and cared for with love. And whether or not you believe they have mystical properties, they bring sparkle and shine to our lives. I'll recommend some to add twinkle and light to each room.

Hang multifaceted feng shui crystals on red strings in the center of each room where you'd like to enliven the chi. Ceiling fans are great places to hang your crystals if you have them—just make sure the strings are long enough so they won't be caught in the fan. Position the loop of the string or cord in the center of the fan so the crystals are hanging down in the center where the pull cord might be.

Spirit Helpers

You can employ spirit energy in each room. We'll touch on everything from Hindu deities of prosperity to ancient goddess beings that can bring you love.

You will learn simple, easy ways to invite high-vibrational deities and guides to bring good energy into each room of the house.

Also, learn about "spirits of place" that preside over land and dwellings. Animal spirit helpers have long been key players in shamanic rituals and  journeys all over the world. I will suggest activities that can connect you with an animal spirit to bring the appropriate energy into your room. I will pass on directional rituals taught to me by my medicine teacher—ways of honoring the flora and fauna of the world along with the "stone people." This ritual was passed down from her teacher and from teacher to student for generations.

Guardian spirits are benevolent helpers that have shared so much love and wisdom with my students, my clients, and myself over the years, and I am so happy to offer what I have learned to you as we make over the energy of your home.

Energy Clearings, Rituals, and Ceremonies

In each room, we will enact an energy ceremony or ritual to optimize its energy and draw your intentions to you. The vibratory frequency of a room is crucial in determining whether it can effectively serve your needs. When we start the journey toward making the most of each room's potential, one of the first things we can do is check in and correct that frequency. So, give these rituals a try and see how you feel in your home afterward—they can go a long way toward making it feel like a strong and sparkly whole!

Taoist Elements and Feng Shui

When evaluating your space, we will study the bagua and employ a number of other techniques from feng shui and Taoist philosophy. We will cover how to achieve peak chi in each room. Plus, we will discuss how to foster yin and yang energy, depending upon which we want to emphasize. Nine is the ultimate power number in feng shui, so get ready for nine tips to power up each room!

BONUS CONTENT ALERT

Hop on to amyleighmercree.com/ healinghomebookresources to get your Healing Home Makeover Journal, to organize what you've done and schedule what you intend to do for each room. You can download this journal and refer back to it as you make over your dwelling.

Vedic Elements, Vastu, and Chakra Healing

There are lots of home hacks to be gleaned from Vedism. As I mentioned earlier in the book, Vastu is the Vedic study of how to best create homes or plan cities, and there is a lot to learn from studying its wisdom. From Vastu to Ayurveda to optimizing chakra energy, there are a number of systems derived from ancient Hinduism

that can be applied to the improvement of the home.

HOLISTIC HEALTH CHECK

In each room, we will do a quick and efficient check to make sure that you are living your healthiest life in your house! This could include removing toxic products, using healthy cleaning solutions, improving air quality, and more.

THE ELEMENTS

Many of these healing systems are seated upon a foundation formed by the five elements as defined in Taoist philosophy. The philosophy of Taoism has no known founder or founding date. It likely began in prehistoric China as a merging of shamanism and nature philosophy. It gained structure in 142 CE with the revelation  of the Tao to Zhang Daoling or Chang Tao-ling by the personified god of the Tao, Taishang Laojun, also known as Lao Tzu. A major feature of Taoism surrounds what it describes as the "five key elements"—wood, fire, earth, metal, and water—and the corresponding belief that each element flows into the next in an ever-renewing creative cycle. Each element has a wide variety of attributes and properties.

Wood

Wood is the beginning, the springtime of the creative cycle. It is the element of innocence and youth, the essence of adventure and new beginnings. It is reminiscent of the way that plant life pushes up through the soil after winter's rest. Wood's movement and motion is upward, bringing us the ability to connect with our true nature and bring our attention to self-expression and self-awareness. The wood element is thought to create a wind in heaven that gives birth to wood upon the earth. The color associated with wood is green. Green and wood essence give people the ability to raise their voices and shout. Wood is also associated with the eyes, sour flavor, and the emotion of anger.

Fire

Wood fuels fire. Fire is associated with summer. It's all about expansion, heat, lightness, brightness, creativity, and growth. It has yang qualities, which indicates masculinity. It is evocative of warm, luxurious expansion. It is all about the heat of the day, the growth and blooming and height of blossoming that occurs in the summer. The fire element beckons us to reach for the sun for our nourishment. Fire element helps us with work and productivity. Its heat helps us play as hard as we work. It's associated with the laughter, humor, singing, dancing, joy, travel, and selfless service fueled by the fire of passion. Fire is about the external, and conversely, the way it enlivens our internal being. It's associated with the color red, the heart, and brightly colored fruits and vegetables that are prevalent in the summer, as well as spicy, pungent, and fiery flavors.

Earth

Fire creates earth. Earth element is associated with the late summer. In the Tao it's about the interchange of all seasons. Late summer is considered a short season in Taoism that consists solely of the last month of summer. It's the time of year that changes from the masculinity of yang to the femininity of yin. It is the transitional time that lies between the expansion of the wood and fire elements and the more inward, cooling fall and winter seasons. The earth element is associated with tranquility. It's the still place where time stops because the transition is happening from fire (summer) to metal (autumn). Earth element is serene, effortless, dreamlike. It fosters unity and what Buddhists refer to as "the middle way," a Buddhist concept that is about avoiding excess and finding the center of one's being.

Earth inhibits excess, which is considered an enemy to wellness in the Tao. It's subtle and present. Earth element is all about the rhythms and cycles of life and the ways in which we find simplicity and harmony within life. It is a place in which we can center ourselves in order to go beyond external conditions. Practices like meditation and breath work are facilitated during earth element times. The earth element is associated with the abdomen, the body's physical center. It is also associated with the spleen, stomach, and pancreas, as it regulates the center of our being. It is the constant part of us that harmonizes the other four elements. It's associated with mildly sweet flavors, and yellow and golden foods. It's also aligned with the mouth and the sense of taste. The earth element is all about moderation.

Metal

Earth forges metal. In Taoism, metal is associated with the season of autumn. It's about harvest time and the cornucopia. It's also a time to turn inward and gather together with community, but also make sure you are nourishing your inner being. It's a time for storing, planning, ideas, food, fuel. It's a time to be warm and nurtured. Studying and planning for the upcoming winter are wise activities.

Everything in nature is always moving, either expanding or contracting, going inward or outward. The metal element is associated with inward and downward movements. Leaves turn, fruit falls, seeds dry. With metal, we have heightened intuition and sensitivity. Trees send their sap downward into their roots, plants and soil dry out. The metal element is associated with the lungs as well as colors like silver and gray, and astringent food flavors. It's also associated with the sense of smell because of its alignment with the lungs. The metal element helps us organize and create structures, mentally and emotionally.

Water

Metal contains water. It creates structure for the unbounded, unrestrained, undulating aspect of the water element. The water element is associated with winter and the end of the Taoist creative cycle. It unifies our being and enables it to become more receptive and introspective and cools the body on the surface while warming it on an internal level. It has a heated internal and a cool external property because the cold and dark of winter drives us inward toward our own warmth. Water brings us time for rest and allows us to refine our spiritual side. The water element is associated with the kidneys and the ears. It is associated with glass, moving water, and, at times, fear. The active principle of the water element creates fame and money. It's an element of reputation and fortune when combined with the other parts of the Tao five elements system. Water is calm on the surface, but like the ocean, it holds dynamic and mysterious depths beneath.

In the Taoist creative cycle, water is the end of the five elements, and it is reincarnated and reborn continually into wood. The cycle begins again and again, with water constantly flowing into wood to help it begin anew. Water feeds wood.

The BAGUA

BAGUA AREA	COLORS	SHAPE & ELEMENT	ASSOCIATED NUMBER	BODY PART
Prosperity & Abundance	Purple and Gold	No shape, Water	8	Hip
Reputation & Fame	Red	Triangular, Pointed, Fire	1	Eye
Love, Sex & Relationships	Pink	Hearts	2	All Major Organs
Creativity & Fertility	White	Circular, Metal	3	Mouth
Helpers & Travel	Grey and Silver	Bells, Metal	5	Head
Career & Dharma	Black	Free-Form, Undulating, Wavy, Water	6	Ear
Skills & Knowledge	Blue	Books	7	Hand
Family & Household Expenses	Green and Wood	Rectangular, Vertical, Columnar, Wood	4	Foot
Health & Surprises	Yellow and Earth Tones	Square, Horizontal, Flat, Earth	9	All Other Body Parts

All people contain aspects of the five elements, but certain properties are usually more prominent on a foundational level. A person's personality and being are usually tilted toward one element above the others.

An interesting pop culture illustration of a person moving from predominantly metal into exploring more of their water element happened when Taylor Swift released her album entitled *Reputation*. It contains songs that explore the edge of good and bad and right and wrong in the crucible of love and romance. When people have an excess of water element, they aren't into the black-and-white constraints that a metal element person would see as right and wrong. At times, water element people display moral ambiguity. In the case of Taylor Swift, *Reputation* was an expression of her creativity that also demonstrated her shift in belief from the black-and-white view of a metal person to the more nuanced feelings often demonstrated by someone with an abundance of water. She expressed parts of metal-element nature creatively in songs past that were more cut and dried insofar as she was the heartbroken person and, in the relationship, the ex-boyfriend behaved poorly, and it was heartbreaking. On the album *Reputation*, there is a song about how it feels so good to do something bad, and she is relishing it. She is exploring the ambiguous nature of the water element in her creative expression there. A lot of charismatic, powerful figures throughout history had a predominant water element—especially those who were able to achieve great things while also negotiating moral ambiguity. So when people are working with the water-element aspects of themselves, the focus needs to be to create enough structure that one behaves with integrity while tapping the charismatic, wealth-creating power of water.

THE BAGUA

The core of using feng shui to better your life revolves around the bagua. We use the bagua to move the chi or energy around the house in the most optimal way. Enhancing the bagua helps us create our lives more effortlessly, because we do not have to expend extra resources to make the energy of our home harmonious. Instead, we set the stage for our lives to flow by setting up the energy of our home to align with our intentions.

Each area of the home is called a *gua* (pronounced "gwa"). There are nine guas in the bagua, and each one governs a different area of our life. If we have intentions for certain parts of our life, then we can use cures to enhance the related gua. Each gua is associated with its own colors, numbers, elements, and other qualities. We use it like a map and envision placing it like an overlay over each floor of the home.

To figure out how to fit the bagua over your home, start by lining up your front door with the bottom of the octagon/bagua. That means that it would align with either the career, the helpful people, or the skills and knowledge area. Some homes may have a missing piece or an additional jutting area of the home that lies outside of the bagua. If you have a missing piece, like for example part of your prosperity area is missing, you can use extra prosperity cures in the closest area to still enhance the chi toward prosperity. Feng shui works because your intention is strong. You can do it!

If you have an additional area that juts outside of the bagua, you can enhance the chi in that area and you can also use a strategically placed mirror to bring the spatial area back into the bagua. Place the mirror just inside the

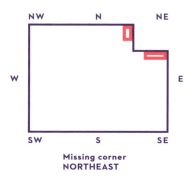

Missing corner
NORTHEAST

bagua so the extra spatial area that is outside of it is reflected in the mirror within the bagua. That is how you bring an extra zone back into the harmonious energy of your home.

Now, let's get a little bit more in-depth about what "feng shui cures" will help you achieve your intentions and create the life of your dreams! In feng shui, we call the changes we make to the environment *cures*. For example, a common cure is hanging a multifaceted crystal from a ceiling fan to disperse the disruptive energy it can create.

Intentional Bagua Cures

There are a number of cures you can use to revitalize the chi of your home. World-renowned bestselling author of my favorite feng shui book, *Move Your Stuff, Change Your Life*, my good friend Karen Rauch Carter says the most important ingredient in any feng shui cure is intention. The following is a list of some ideas for cures for each area of your home. A little goes a long way, so you don't have to do all of them at once. Simply set an intention while making the changes specified below, and then as you physically change the space, state your intention aloud.

PROSPERITY: Anything purple or red is a power color and can bring extra excitement and energy to an area. Green is a symbol of money and growth, and you could include adding real dollar bills to an altar or other space. Also helpful: anything gold (I love golden Buddha statues, for example!); any symbols that remind you of wealth and abundance; anything symbolizing water, especially if it's moving (such as a painting or photo of a rushing river). Glass symbolizes water in feng shui, so it's also helpful in this area.

FAME AND REPUTATION: Fire and anything symbolizing it can help you achieve fame if that's what you want in life! Candles, fireplaces, lanterns, lights and lamps, lots of red, and anything triangular (especially if it is tall), pointed objects, pyramids—all are great. This is the only gua where a cactus would be

recommended! Green, because of what it symbolizes, will feed the energy of this area. Consider placing your television in the fame and reputation gua, as well as vertically oriented items and pictures, animals and things made from animals, and pictures or symbols of celebrities or people you admire who have the reputation you want. When you are attempting to increase fame in a particular room, it's a good place to display awards, diplomas, professional licenses, or anything associated with height, such as pictures of mountains or the sun.

RELATIONSHIPS: Where you want to encourage strong relationships, consider adding round mirrors, two candles, fresh flowers, and lots of pink or red. A room meant to be the home of a treasured relationship isn't a bad place in which to store undergarments and anything sensual. It's also an excellent place to display symbols that mean love to you, animal prints or images (a painting or photo of two lovebirds, for example), images of fireworks, or other romantic symbols.

CREATIVITY: When you need a space for your creative endeavors, choose decorations or furniture made of metal, anything white or round, or even things with a little bit of yellow. Objects that represent earth (which feeds the metal element) can be beneficial, including stones, plants potted in soil, and pottery made from clay. As can toys and games, things that remind you of the happiness of childhood, or bright lights, which equal bright ideas in this gua. A metal bell or symbols of children can also be good additions. It may seem obvious, but consider putting your art studio or finished pieces of art or crafts in this area for added inspiration!

HELPERS AND TRAVEL: This area's energy can be improved with lots of

Feng Shui Bagua Map For Your Home

PROSPERITY & ABUNDANCE:
wealth-building, fun money, investments, long term financial health

FAME & REPUTATION:
personal branding, business identity, accolades, how you are seen by the world, receiving award

LOVE, SEX & RELATIONSHIPS:
harmony in all relationships, including work and home, passion and sensuality, feeling the joy of love, unconditional self-love

FAMILY & HOUSEHOLD EXPENSES:
security of the family unit, familial bonding, money to sustain the members of the household day to day, resources to pay bills and take care of basic needs

HEALTH & SURPRISES:
vitality and energy for life, overall good health, resolving specific health concerns, mind-body wellness, optimizing the body to age well, happy surprises, laughterr

CREATIVITY & FERTILITY:
innovative ideas, out of the box thinking and problem solving, artistic endeavors, creating life and having children, fertility optimization, the innocence and sparkle of the childlike being, staying inspired through all phases of life

SKILLS & KNOWLEDGE:
being an expert in your field, adding new abilities to enhance your life, learning, schooling, wisdom, awareness of self and vastness

CAREER & DHARMA:
exceling and being promoted in your chosen field, living your life's purpose, raises in via career, building a successful business, reaching new heights through meaningful work, right livelihood

HELPERS & TRAVEL:
aligning with the right people to assist you in your goals, connecting with spirit guides, manifesting luxurious travel, adventure, peak experiences, voyages, exploration, anderlust

THE FRONT DOOR

silver, metal, gray, symbols of helpful beings, religious objects, bells, images of hands, water or images of water, symbols of places you would like to go, maps, and globes.

CAREER: To give your career a boost in a particular area of the house, water of any kind, even if just a picture, is extremely helpful. The color black, undulating shapes and free-form items, mirrors, glass, metal, white items, and round items are also great. And don't forget symbols of the career and life path that you desire (I like to use best-selling books by authors I admire!).

SKILLS AND KNOWLEDGE: In this area, add lots of blue, books, lights to illuminate the mind, food to fuel your brain, symbols of wisdom, symbols of mentors or wise people, metal, water, black, wood, green, meditation items, altars of gratitude, and symbols of the skills or knowledge you would like to have.

FAMILY: Add to the loving family energy in this area with lots of green, wood, rectangular objects, columnar objects, water, black, and undulating forms.

HEALTH: If you have an area of the home where you'd like to increase the energy of good health, add lots of yellow, gold, earth tones, and square forms or objects. Earth and symbols of earth, things made of earth, fruit, funny items, horizontal items, flat items, images of the stars and sun, and anything that adds a little bit of fire (whether literally, like a candle, or figuratively, like an object symbolizing fire) are great.

BAGUA MAP

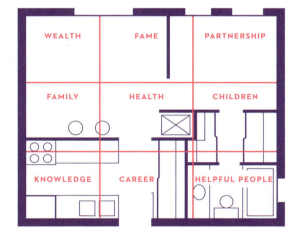

The Vedic Five Elements and Doshas

The Vedas are a group of four ancient Sanskrit texts originating in India. They are the oldest Hindu texts and are estimated to have been written between 1500 and 500 BCE. It is from these texts of Vedic wisdom that Vastu, Ayurveda, Yoga, and Vedic astrology are derived. In Hinduism, similar to Taoism, there are five elements based upon ancient knowledge of cosmology and energy: ether, air, fire, water, and earth.

Ether

Akasha is the Sanskrit name for "ether," indicating empty space and the absence of any resistance. It is the beginning in the Vedic cosmology. Ether existed before the other elements. Its essence is pervasiveness and interconnection.

Air

Vayu is the Sanskrit name for "air." Out of Akasha (ether) there was Vayu (air). It is the essence of movement and is sometimes referred to as wind. Its properties are cold, dry, rough, and light.

Fire

The Sanskrit name of "fire" is Agni. It is born of ether and air. Air moving in ether creates friction and heat and yields fire. In Vedic wisdom, fire is evocative of radiance and transformation and is associated with the eyes because it is visible.

Water

"Water" is called Jala or Ap in Sanskrit. In Vedic creation, fire causes density in the air, and water is born. It is associated with cohesion, dilution, and our sense of taste. It's considered soft, slow, and cooling, and is part of all of the bodily fluids in Ayurveda.

Earth

Prithivi is the Sanskrit name for "earth." It is a combination of the four previous elements plus cosmic dust to create the densest and heaviest element. It associated with inertia, stability, and resistance to movement. It is also thought to be connected to the sense of smell.

In Ayurveda, the five elements are thought to combine to create *doshas*, which teach us how to create and maintain equilibrium in our bodies and beings. The doshas consist of Vata (air/ether), Pitta (fire/water), and Kapha (water/earth). Later in our journey we will connect the Vedic elements and doshas with your home and learn how to strengthen their energies and regulate them so that they flow smoothly.

CHAKRAS

As you may know, the chakra system that we hear about today, in which rainbow colors and a collection of properties are associated with seven energy centers in our body, is the most recent iteration of many different theories of chakra energy centers originally developed in the Vedic culture. Beginning 2,500 to 4,000 years ago, many systems have been used to describe the chakras. There have been chakras of varying colors and anywhere from 1 to 144 chakras recorded in different Vedic and other texts. For our purposes, we will use a format originally popularized by Alice A. Bailey and Helena P. Blavatsky in the nineteenth century, which emphasizes seven chakras. However, I will also be integrating concepts from other writings on the chakras that may be useful in understanding their impact upon the physical space in which you live.

THE SEVEN NATIVE AMERICAN ELEMENTS AND DIRECTIONS

Twenty-six years ago, I met my medicine teacher, Laurie Levity, for the first time. She was trained in an oral tradition by her medicine teacher, Twila, who was trained by a Native American memory keeper. This oral tradition has been passed down from teacher to student for many generations, and I continue to pass along their teachings and traditions in shamanism classes and to my apprentices. This book includes some of that wisdom, including thoughts on the Native American medicine wheel, or sacred hoop, which has been used by a number of different tribes over many years, as well as the importance of the cardinal directions and their connection to the elements on this earth.

The Medicine Wheel

The medicine wheel outlines the seven directions, plus Mother Earth, Father Sky, and the Spirit Tree. When we work with the grandmothers of the seven directions, we use the construct of the medicine wheel. We enter it in the East and travel next to the South, then the West, then the North, then to the center, where we begin by honoring the elements below, then the

elements above, and then the elements all around. Here is the way the medicine wheel breaks down when we look at the elemental language that we will later use to heal, order, and improve the energy of your home.

AIR/EAST

Air is the beginning. It is the East and the dominion of Golden Eagle Woman, grandmother of new beginnings, dawn, springtime, and birth.

FIRE/SOUTH

Next in the medicine wheel, we move to the South and the fire element and the heat of high noon. This area is presided over by three grandmothers: Grandmother Green Mouse Woman, Grandmother Coyote Woman, and Grandmother Butterfly Woman. The fire element is associated with summer and ecstatic life.

WATER/WEST

In our journey around the medicine wheel, we now move to the West and the domain of cleansing and dreams. Two grandmothers watch over this section: Grandmother Black Bear Woman and Grandmother Green Frog Woman. This element is symbolic of autumn and dusk. It clears us of our density and beckons us into the cave of dreams.

EARTH/NORTH

The North is next, presided over by Grandmother White Buffalo Woman. Here we connect with the element of earth and the essences of alchemy and wisdom. We feel the stillness of deep winter and the quiet of midnight.

BELOW

When we walk the medicine wheel coming from the North we step into the center and crouch down, connecting with that which is a below us. There we connect with the Grandmother Path Keeper. This element is more abstract, evocative of the dualistic nature of creation. We will use this in our journey to harmonize our home in this book.

Grandmother Path Keeper helps us stay on the good red road and guides our path. The good red road is symbolic of integrity. And so, this element called below is related to our integrity and our earth walk.

ABOVE

We are still in the center of the medicine wheel and we rise and reach our arms up above to connect with the essence known as Grandmother Sky Blanket and Grandmother Star Nation. These are personifications of the atmosphere, clouds, and cosmos. The above is an element that connects us with outer space and the atmosphere, and it helps shape our expanded worldview.

ALL AROUND

Last, as we stand in the center of the medicine wheel, we offer our gratitude and connection to that which is all around us. It is comprised of the plant people, the animal people, the stone people, and all of the nonphysical beings that inhabit this dimension and beyond. This oral tradition is part of the guiding essence that shapes our existence. We call this grandmother the Great Spirit or the Great Mystery. She is the goddess and is all things. My medicine teacher, Laurie, would do a beautiful ritual with all of these grandmothers and these directions that was passed down from her teacher, and from teacher to student in an oral tradition for many generations. At the end, when she offered thanks to all of the directions, she would say, ". . . to the wingeds, the four leggeds, the bird people, the stone people, the plant people . . ." The approach she learned from her teacher was holistic and included appreciations of all of the parts of this earth, and I hope that you will continue to thank the energy on this planet as you work with the energy within your dwelling.

These are some of the elemental systems' wisdom that we will be drawing upon as we create your healing home. We want to create the healthiest, most nourishing place for you and anyone with whom you live.

If you'd like to hear audio interviews I recorded with my beloved medicine teacher, check them out online at amyleighmercree.com/ healinghomebookresources.

A Note on Clutter

Generally speaking, clutter is the enemy of energy flow in the home. We almost always want to clear clutter! There are only a few situations in which clutter is helpful—for example, it could be supportive if you've been through an extreme experience that is still too intense to process. In that case, a little bit of soft clutter in the form of clothes, linens, and things like that can bring yin energy into the space. Because yin is associated with the feminine and it brings comfort, it could prevent you from becoming overwhelmed with your circumstances and can be a useful buffer until you are feeling more energized and ready to deal with your experience. If you've been dealing with overactive, intense feelings, they might be too yang, and a little bit of extra padding in the home could be *temporarily* helpful. Still, remember to be aware of when that padding has become stuck chi—energy in the form of unhelpful patterns. That's when you know you'll have to deal with the mess for your own mental and spiritual well-being.

In most situations, cleaning and removing clutter creates energy flow. There's no way around it—clutter is in the way! So here are a few tips for taking the first steps to get rid of it.

» Are there books piling up that you'll never read? Give them away.

» Are there clothes you don't wear? Donate them.

» Piles of receipts that you don't need? Toss them.

» Old makeup that is over twelve months old? It is likely too old to use and could be harboring bacteria, so toss it.

» CDs that you can't play on any computer you have? Consider donating them to a nursing home or library or recycle them at CD Recycling Center of America or Green Disk.

» Old electronics, like phones, laptops, and tablets, that are outdated? Wipe them clean and then do a factory reset to erase things you have forgotten are stored, like saved passwords. Then donate them. You can check out World Computer Exchange or Dell Reconnect. Or recycle them. Call2Recycle.org has options for most areas.

Take some time going through each room, pacing yourself, and ask yourself, Do you need or love each item you see? If the answer is no, toss it.

If you're struggling with debt, clutter will make it worse. When we tolerate clutter, energy doesn't flow. If energy is not flowing, it may cause obstacles that will keep you from earning or keeping money. It could also affect your romantic life, your career, and really any other aspect of your life—prosperity isn't just relegated to money in the bank. Open space in your home and you make room for new energy and flow. Get rid of stacks of papers, old magazines, old files. And don't underestimate the power of a digital cleanse! Clean out the unnecessary files and photos on your computer regularly. The more order you maintain, the more that good energy and prosperity can find you.

A good rule of thumb when it comes to clutter is 50-50: aim for 50 percent open space in your home, with 50 percent in use and occupied by the trappings of your everyday life. Start by visualizing the three-dimensional shape of the room you are in now, edge to edge, floor to ceiling, top to bottom. For example, I am in my office. So in this case I picture the room like a rectangular box. Fifty percent or more of this room should be empty space. Now expand that thinking out to each floor of your home. More than 50 percent of the total space should be open.

If a room feels like a bummer, rehab its energy by cleaning it! Dust, wipe all surfaces down, and don't forget to clean the corners! Corners collect energy, so it's especially important to make sure you clean them regularly.

Clutter makes us feel like we are carrying more of a burden than we actually are, particularly if you are taking on the lion's share of cleaning responsibility while the rest of your family is uninvolved. Encourage everyone in the home to clean. Even the smallest children can help put away their shoes, sort laundry, hang up clothes and coats, and eliminate piles of toys by putting them back on a shelf or in a toy box. I have to confess I struggle with this process. As an ADHD person, I'm great at blocking out piles of clutter when I'm prioritizing other activities. I'm especially good at ignoring things like baskets of laundry. So I work hard at making sure to notice them, and I encourage you to do the same—the effect on the energy flow in your home will be palpable!

For instance, when clutter is at the waist level, for example on dirty counters and in drawers that are too full, it emits too much yin energy. Too much yin dulls your senses, makes you sleepy, and doesn't bring you the opportunities you desire. So clear the clutter today!

A beneficial way to break up the energy of clutter is to hang a wind chime over an area where it accumulates. Tap these chimes daily to break up the clutter's stagnant energy, making it easier for you to purge messes and clear the space. You can also turn on ceiling fans temporarily to break up stuck chi in a room.

As you clear clutter, have a specific intention that can be as simple as, "I now release any stagnant energy to make space for new, fresh, high-vibrational energy and opportunities." You can also ask yourself as you are getting rid of clutter, "What do I want to replace this with energetically?" The arrangement of items and energy in our homes has a powerful effect on our lives.

I want to hear your clutter-clearing stories! Post a before and after picture of the room or closet on Facebook or Instagram and tag me @amyleighmercree and use our hashtag #thehealinghome and I will repost your success!

"Good luck on your clutter-clearing journey!"

VOCs, EMFs, OMG! (Create Your Healthy House Chemical Clear-Out!)

Many of the techniques in this book address the spiritual and energetic components of your home first, but I would be remiss to neglect actual products that can cause adverse health effects. Every year, more research is done into the effects of unhealthy chemicals used within the home, so a chemical cleanout making sure you've gotten rid of them is a good use of your time. Here are some steps you can take.

VOCs (Volatile Organic Compounds)

Volatile organic compounds, also known as VOCs, are a group of widely used ingredients in household products. They are quickly evaporated or emitted as gas at room temperature from certain solid and liquid products containing them. VOCs can be released as gas at room temperature (68°F to 72°F). VOCs off-gas into the air we breathe.

The Minnesota Department of Health identified some of the common VOCs present in our daily lives as follows: benzene, ethylene glycol, formaldehyde, methylene chloride, tetrachloroethylene, toluene, xylene, and 1,3-butadiene.

The US Environmental Protection Agency indicated that concentrations of VOCs are greater indoors than outdoors, where they can be dispersed. According to Berkeley Lab, indoor sources of VOCs are present partially suspended in the air and partially absorbed (or attached on the outside surface) on indoor surfaces, such as walls and furniture. So open the windows daily to air out the house!

An important subgroup of VOCs of which we should be aware are semi-volatile organic compounds, or SVOCs. Berkeley Lab specifies that SVOCs have a higher molecular weight and a higher boiling point than other VOCs, which means they are released as gas more quickly.

They are primarily present in building and decorating materials such as vinyl wallpaper or vinyl flooring; building materials and furniture with flame retardants (a chemical substance applied to combustible materials to prevent them from starting a fire or to slow the spread of fire); and pesticides. Although you are not applying flame retardants to your own furniture or pesticides to your own food, these items are often present in the home because they are on what you have brought in. Awareness is the first step, and then you can reduce your exposure by being conscious of what you add to your homes and replace certain items with more healthy options over time. The EPA's studies found that using VOC-containing products can cause exposure to pollutants. After use, emitted VOCs can persist in the air at elevated concentrations.

The EPA reported that VOC inhalation whether over a short- or long-term period can have negative

Household sources of VOCs:

Building Materials	Home & Personal Care Products	Human Activities
Paints	Air fresheners	Smoking
Varnishes	Fragrance-scented candles	Dry cleaning
Caulks	Cleaning products	Photocopiers
Adhesives	Cosmetics	Cooking
Carpet & vinyl flooring	Fuel oil & gasoline	Burning wood in
Composite wood	(both when used or stored)	any capacity where
products		you inhale the
Upholstery & foam		fumes

health effects. The chart on page XLII shows the findings of the Minnesota Department of Health.

Inspect your home for common sources of VOCs, including unused chemicals. Read the labels. Check furnishings, like carpets and upholsteries made from composite wood (usually a mixture of wood, plastic, and straw), as they tend to off-gas VOCs.

Start noticing the products in your home that have added fragrance that is not pure essential oil, as it can be hazardous and may cause asthma and allergies in some people. These might be cleaning products, makeup, toiletries, shampoo, and scented candles. You can dispose of those via the regular trash removal process. Some other VOC-containing products, like treated wood or carpets, can be a bit trickier. When you find those VOC-containing products, remove them but do not dispose of them with your household garbage! There are proper disposal methods for toxic chemicals. Contact your local municipality or local waste management office to find the best way in your area.

Consider purchasing low-VOC options for paints and furnishing and other home products as much as possible. Also, look for building materials that have had more time to off-gas instead of getting new stock from the storeroom, if possible.

Allowing a good flow of air in your home will help reduce the concentration of VOCs. This can be done by opening windows or doors as well as using fans.

EMFs

Cell phones, tablets, computers, and home appliances including microwave ovens radiate invisible electromagnetic waves, or EMFs. The National Cancer Institute defined EMFs as invisible waves of energy (radiation) produced by electricity. The National Cancer Institute explained that an electrical field is produced by voltage, which acts as a pressure that pushes

Home Hazards

Short Term Exposure Effects	Long Term Exposure Impact
Eye, nose & throat irritation Headaches Nausea/vomiting Dizziness Worsening of asthma symptoms	Cancer Liver & kidney damage Central nervous system damage

electrons through a wire. Therefore, as voltage increases, so does an electrical field. A magnetic field is the flow of current through an electrical device. According to the National Cancer Institute, electrical fields can be effortlessly hindered by walls and other objects. In contrast, magnetic fields can pass through buildings, different materials, and even living things.

In 2017, a study by Magda Havas of Trent School of the Environment (Trent University in Canada) found evidence of cellular damage caused by nonionizing radiation, which is emitted by cell phones and many other home sources. Her research highlights that nonionizing radiation interferes with the oxidative repair of our cells, which can lead to cancer.

Another finding on the effects of cell phones and other wireless devices on children was conducted by Anthony Miller and his team in 2019 from Dalla Lana School of Public Health, University of Toronto. The study discovered that a cell phone near a child's head exposes deep brain structures to greater radiation, including the skull's bone marrow. Moreover, studies have also shown that men keeping cell phones in their pockets are at risk of lower sperm counts and impaired sperm motility.

Measure EMFs in the home with a gaussmeter by Meterk and TriField. Check the areas where you spend the most time. Position your sleeping area in a low-EMF area. Do not sit right next to your wi-fi router for long periods of time. Keep your phone away from you when not in use, especially during sleep. Practice lessening the time of phone use. Use wired earbuds as opposed to wireless. According to the National Cancer Institute, a distance of twelve to twenty inches from the computer screen has slightly lower radiation. Maintaining at least a one-foot distance from most appliances is also helpful.

There are lots of EMF-blocking blankets on the market. They are a great idea if you sit with your laptop in your lap frequently. They are often recommended for pregnant women to protect their babies. It's also a fabulous idea to use them to protect your internal organs.

Because the science on the effects of EMFs is evolving so quickly, I have included an up-to-date resource list on amyleighmercree.com/healinghomebookresources so I can share the latest findings with you. Nicolas Pineault's book *The Non-Tinfoil Guide to EMFs* contains lots of helpful information, too.

Other Chemicals

VOCs and EMFs are endocrine-system disruptors. There are other endocrine-disrupting chemicals that can be found in cosmetics, house cleaners, and personal-care products.

PHTHALATES are colorless and odorless endocrine-disrupting chemicals. They help make products durable and stable. Besides being present in many personal care and household products, phthalates are also used in building and construction materials; wire and cable; automotive parts such as car interiors and seat covers; footwear such as rain boots; and textiles for durable clothing and luggage. Clinical studies in the years 2017 and 2020 (by Claudia Campanale and team; Sailas Benjamin and team; and Sudipta Dutta and team) reported the adverse effects of phthalate ingestion, mainly in its epigenomic consequences to humans. Phthalates cause alteration of physical DNA structure, which may lead to diseases, such as reproductive and developmental toxicities, including cancer.

PARABENS are used as preservatives and antimicrobial agents in cosmetics, personal care products, food, and pharmaceutical products. It was reported in a 2018 study by Rahul Tade and team that parabens are easily absorbed in the skin and gut and can be excreted in the urine. Accumulation of parabens may increase the risk of breast cancer. A 2020 study proved that parabens persist in the breast tissue of breast cancer patients. The study pointed out that the estrogenic and xenoestrogenic (fake estrogen) properties of parabens play a role in developing breast cancer. Moreover, as an endocrine disruptor, parabens affect all of the endocrine glands, including the thyroid and adrenal glands. Like phthalates, parabens cause reproductive problems in both men and women, such as by reducing the concentration of sperm, and shortening menstrual periods.

BPA (bisphenol A) is used in food and beverages. BPA is often present in the plastic lining within food and beverage cans. BPA is commonly found in plastic food containers and plastic bottles. The chemical enters the body through ingestion since not all of the BPA is sealed in the container; some of it may go through the food or drink it holds.

A study in 2019 by Anna Abraham and Paromita Chakraborty found that, even in low consumption, BPAs can still stimulate cellular responses such as by altering hormones and metabolism. Another notable finding was exposed in 2020, by Vicente Mustieles and Mariana Fernandez and their team at the University of Granada, Spain, linking prenatal BPA exposure and a child's brain and behavior. The study reported that the brain is one of the most sensitive organs to be disrupted by BPA, even below safe doses by the European Food Safety Authority. So, here are a few ways to reduce endocrine-disruptor exposure:

1. Do not microwave food using plastic containers or plastic-coated paper products. Phthalates, when heated, can leach from containers into your food.

2. Buy phthalate-free and paraben-free products, including toothbrushes, toys, food storage containers, dishes, hair care products, sunscreen, and cosmetics.

3. Choose fragrance-free products unless they are exclusively scented with therapeutic-grade essential oils. Since you won't find the word *phthalates* on the product label, just try to avoid the terms *fragrance*, *perfume*, or *parfum*, as they often indicate the presence of phthalates. It's worth it to look for therapeutic-grade essential oils— they're 100 percent good for you and will delight your senses!

4. Products with the recycling codes 3 and 7 may contain phthalates or BPA. Instead, look for recycling-safe codes 1, 2, and 5.

5. Invest in water filters. Granular, activated carbon filters can help in removing phthalates from PVC water pipes. Although it can be costly, a nanofiltration system is a more reliable way to filter out phthalates. Check ewg. org for water filtration information and check your bathing and drinking water at the Environmental Working Group's Tap Water Database.

6. Think about buying glass, wood, and stainless-steel containers, utensils, cups, and bowls for the kitchen to reduce your interaction with plastics.

PART 1

The
FRONT
DOOR

If you're looking for a sign, this is it! This section is the first step toward optimizing your home and creating good vibes in every single room. However, before you enter the threshold, there are a few foundational things to consider. The front door is important both as a metaphor for the beginning of this process and as the physical truth that the view behind the door is the first thing you and your guests will see when entering your home. How can we make this space welcoming and bright, happy and secure? Welcome to this section of the book as we begin to create the healing home about which you have always dreamed!

FOYER

It has been a long day filled with work commitments, emails, texts, calls, noise, demands on your time and attention, and lots of stimulation. You approach your front door, and as soon as you step into your home, you relax. The warm, inviting smell of cardamom essential oil fills your nose and lights up your senses. The golden setting sun flickers across the foyer walls. You are surrounded by the greenery of vibrant houseplants. All is right with the world—thank goodness you're home!

When you enter the space where you live—whether that's the front door of your studio apartment or the sprawling entrance inside the double doors of your mansion—that first impression is going to color your impression of your entire space. And that doesn't just go for you: your family and your guests will also take away a lot from this first interaction.

That means that, in terms of making over the energy of your home, the foyer is a wonderful place to start.

A good first step lies in the bagua, which we introduced on page XX. The bagua can give you some initial feedback on how to organize your space. When it comes to your foyer, the first step is to take the grid and place it over an approximate rendering of the first floor of your home. Start by lining up your front door with the bottom of the octagon. This will help you understand if it aligns with career, helpful people, or skills and knowledge area. You will use those cures by the front door plus extra career cures.

The entrance to the home lets the good energy flow in and enlivens all parts of the house. Whether you have a foyer there or the front door opens into one of the other rooms, pay special attention to that area.

THE ENERGY OF THE FOYER

When you enter your home, a powerful alchemy occurs. The energy of your being combines with the energy of your home to create frequencies, or flavors, of chi. For example, if you feel down as you enter the front door but the energy of that area is uplifting, you will be uplifted, too. Because the front door is where most of the chi that enlivens the space metaphorically flows in, we want to infuse it well. The words *feng shui* are loosely translated to mean "the energy of fortune." That essence is perfect for the foyer. I have had many clients over the years who have added an element of luxuriousness or a symbol of prosperity to the front door area and have seen an upswing in their careers and bank accounts. Pay close attention to the front door area and make sure it is clear of obstacles and clutter, so good opportunities can find you.

Healing Power Mantras

All avenues are open for goodness, prosperity, and joy to enter this house!
Welcome to the good life!
Beauty and joy flow into this space through the front door. All chi that
the inhabitants need to live in ease, joy, and vibrant health
cascades in and creates pleasure and wonder for all within.
My heart's desires come to me easily and effortlessly and life is easy and fun.

AROMATHERAPY FOR THE FOYER

The first impression your home provides should be one of welcome and friendliness, good health and abundance. Scent can support that feeling—it can set the mood for the day and make guests feel happy to be in your home. Fir essential oil is a wonderful scent for the foyer. It has an uplifting and stimulating presence. Fun fact: it is also helpful in tonifying kidney energy. Spruce essential oil can keep the chi moving into the house, bringing in energy so that you, your family, and your guests will be able to accomplish great things.

FRONT DOOR
GOOD FORTUNE SPRITZ

Spray this blend onto and around your front door to bring good fortune to all who enter. You can also use this on your body as a perfume, provided you use therapeutic-grade essential oils.

Ingredients

Spring or distilled water to almost fill up a
4–6 ounce nonplastic bottle of your choice
15 drops of fir essential oil
10 drops of spruce essential oil
5 drops of cardamom essential oil

Place all the ingredients into a clean spray bottle and mix well. Shake well before use. While this is amazing as a good luck, front door spray, you can also use it to spritz your countertops, shower walls, sink, faucets, towels, and washcloths.

FOYER

HOUSEPLANTS FOR THE FOYER

The cast-iron plant, or *Aspidistra elatior*, can help remove harmful chemicals like formaldehyde, toluene, and xylene from the air. This plant is named *cast-iron* because it is super hardy: it can live in many different settings and is a resilient and adaptable indoor plant. It does well in nearly full shade, so if your foyer isn't well lit, consider a cast-iron plant. Just keep in mind that variegated varieties need more light than solid green ones. Invite this plant into your home to share its strength and robust countenance with the inhabitants.

If you're looking for a flower arrangement to add to your foyer or front hallway, peonies are a beautiful choice. With their gorgeous, flamboyant blooms, they invite sweetness and prosperity to your home. Peonies bring an exquisite profusion of beauty into the home and set the stage for an abundant life full of good fortune. Let your peony friends invite the good life into your home!

CRYSTALS FOR THE FOYER

Sprinkle a few minerals throughout the foyer or near the front door to enliven your space and infuse it energy with prosperity and joy. Set the stage for good vibes in your home.

JADE: This stone magnetizes abundance. Harness its ability to pull wealth into your home and life. Placed near the front door, it flavors your life with luxury. Set your jade on a shelf or piece of furniture with intention, and state, "I am wrapped in luxury and enjoy being rich and prosperous."

BLACK TOURMALINE: This is a protective stone that is excellent for repelling negative energy from the home. It imparts peace of mind and serenity and is grounding. Black tourmaline will keep away unwanted guests and invite only good energy inside.

Spirit Helpers

To create a welcoming space for your foyer, you'll need to invoke a powerful energy that can make a strong impression. The benevolent goddess Astarte can help you set a high vibrational stage for the rest of the home. Astarte is associated with the evening star, also known as the planet Venus. Astarte is the Mesopotamian incarnation of the queen of heaven and her reach is far and wide, once including the Phoenicians (as Ashtart), some Egyptians, and the Canaanites (as Asherah). She helps her devotees with wealth building, romance, love, sexuality, pleasure, beauty, fertility, and inner peace through self-acceptance. Her sacred flower is the apple blossom. When you cut an apple in half horizontally, the inside arrangement of seeds forms a star. This plant and symbol are widely associated with a-STAR-te, one of the original queens of heaven.

Meditation to Invoke the Energy of Astarte

State the following invocation aloud inside, near the front door: "Dearest Astarte, please magnetize happiness, prosperity, optimum health, harmony, fun, and ease in this home. Open the doors wide for high-vibrational energy to enter and pull it into the home for the highest good of the inhabitants. Thank you for enhancing our lives. It is done."

Astarte has come to you today to impart her sense of wonder and appreciation of the mysteries of life. She will bring you good fortune if you ask. She teaches that good fortune is for all, and it is your birthright to receive it. You are worthy of abundance, success, love, and all you desire. Astarte will gently and lovingly remind you of this truth. Good fortune is not mystical or magical: it is created via your frequency. Astarte will tirelessly work to attune your home's frequency, because she can never tire. She is a being outside of duality, capable of bringing you to higher and higher frequencies. Tell her "Yes!" today and ask her to guide you.

If you choose, you can give her total permission to make your life easy, happy, and prosperous. Tell her that you give your consent for her to affect your life for the better and change your circumstances in greater and greater ways. You can choose to use your free will to ask spirit guides for help. They cannot impose their desires on us and will use their energies to help us be well and happy if we ask. So, ask! Astarte is here in the room with you and sending you immense love and healing. She is attracting what you desire and can bring it to you in quantities larger than you could imagine. She will help you live your life's purpose and find meaning and joy in all you do. Accept Astarte's help with gratitude. You deserve it all.

Spirits of Place

Call in the spirits who govern the land over which your front door is built. Ask them for wealth, joy, ease, and clear high-vibrational energy. State aloud in front of the front door, "I ask that all that transpires in this space be for the highest good of all life and in accordance with universal natural law, helping all and harming none. Please bring clear  high-vibrational light into this space to create a place that joyfully aligns with my heart's desires."

Animal Helpers

To bring abundance and happiness into the home through its main portal, envision a school of beautiful multicolored fish swimming in and bringing prosperous water energy. They will flow into the space and fill it with light and life. Water is synonymous with prosperity and magnetism in Taoism, and it is meant to flow into the front door. The spirit of schooling, shiny fish will enliven the space and bring abundance and joy. You can picture these fish as golden for prosperity, if that's what you wish for. Allow the splendid idea of animal guardians to delight your imagination. You can say aloud, "I welcome the benevolent spirits of joyful, wealth-bringing lucky fish into my space with gratitude. Thank you for your presence, dear friends."

Golden Door Protection Ritual

The only materials this ritual requires are your brain and being! It is based completely upon intention, and I have seen its power with my clients for twenty years. With concentrated focus, we can create an energetic result. Energy follows thought. Matter follows energy. We will apply intention and focus to enact a desired result. Intention and focus are two key ingredients in the art and science of shamanism, which I have been teaching for over twenty years.

Position yourself inside the house near the front door. Begin by saying the following invocation aloud: "I ask that all that transpires in this ritual be for the highest good of all life and in accordance with universal natural law, helping all and harming none. I welcome the presence of my highest vibrational spirit guides and thank them for their help. I ask that I be protected fully during this process. I now connect with my higher self. I come into alignment with my higher self and feel the truth in my being that I *am* my higher self. I am my higher self."

Now, from the space where you set a very clear intention, look at the front door from the inside. See the shape and size in your mind's eye. Now close your eyes and say aloud, "Only that which is of the light may enter this home." How does that feel? Look at the front door again.

While looking at the front door state those words again: "Only that which is of the light may enter this home."

Next, we're going to create an energetic filter and place it over the front door. This filter will remain in place until you either consciously remove it or move out of the home. That is now your intention and so it will be. State aloud, "I ask my spirit guides and higher self to join me in placing a high-vibrational golden mesh filter over the front door. This will screen out all negative energy and density and keep it from entering this home. I am very grateful for the help of my many benevolent guides in this process."

Now, bring your eyes to the top of the doorframe. In a moment, you will picture the gold mesh attaching to the top of the doorframe so it's outside of the home and enclosing the front door. Think of this mesh like an energetic screen. It allows only good vibrations and positive energy into the home and keeps dense energy out. Be aware, this will potentially change who enters your house. If someone is going to bring dense energy into the home and deposit it there, they will end up canceling or changing their plans. This is a fabulous gift for which we can be grateful. It is positive and helpful. When you make a commitment to high-vibrational living and good health, sometimes things in your life will shuffle and reposition themselves. Understand that that's for your highest good and is a positive change. Sometimes change makes us apprehensive, but we can't escape it, because change is constant. By applying and relentlessly focusing

FOYER

on high-vibrational living, you can create a life of vitality and well-being.

Bring your eyes to the top of the doorframe and picture your higher self and all of your benevolent guides outside the front door gathered around you in a circle. Together you will strengthen this gold mesh filter. You can envision this process happening, or you can even walk up to the door, reach your hands up to the doorframe, and pretend that you're pulling it down from above. It's your choice. So picture gold mesh attaching at the top of the outside of the doorframe. Picture it unrolling straight down. Notice that it is wide enough to cover the entire doorframe and front door. Unroll the gold mesh straight down over the front door on the outside. Watch your guides help you do this. See how shiny and bright this gold mesh is. Keep unrolling it straight down over the front door and bring it all the way down to the ground and tuck the gold mesh in under the bottom of the front doorframe. See how it perfectly covers the entire doorframe, even the sides and edges. Look at the shiny, bright golden mesh over the front door. Notice how it sparkles. State aloud, "This golden mesh is infinite, eternal, and will remain until I consciously remove it or completely vacate the premises and move out of this home. It and my guides shall protect this home and only allow that which is of the light to enter. It is done."

If you have a back or side door for which you would like to enact this practice, you may. Now, say thank you to all of your guides and your higher self for their presence and protection.

FENG SHUI IN THE FOYER

The front door is the portal by which much of the chi in the house enters. We can use that power to ramp up our lives by consciously constructing the energy of the area to magnify our desires. You have the power to create your life. You are the architect of your reality and you can use your home to draw to you what you want. You're powerful! A consumer-driven society might not want you to realize that, since it is more profitable for corporations to make you want to shrink yourself or fix yourself to be better by using their products, but you already have what you need. The raw, sheer, energetic power within your body and being can help you reach your goals without spending a single dime. As a medical intuitive for the past twenty years, one of the main things I teach is that your body is a self-regulating wonder. That is because you are a creator, and you have direct access to universal life force at all times. In this book, what we do is consciously direct that life force.

Feng Shui Foyer Cures

These cures will give you a framework for using the force of your own mind and body. Try adding one to your foyer, and when you've had a chance to digest how it has changed the space energetically, continue adding as many as you'd like.

1. **The front door is a place for the water element according to the Taoist bagua. This area energizes the careers of the people living in the house and especially whomever participated in placing the cures.**

Moving water is the symbol of this energy, which prompts cascading waterfalls of career success and opportunities. A fountain or an aquarium produces this effect, as does art that depicts rivers, waterfalls, and moving-water elements. I created an abstract painting for this area using blues, blacks, and whites and then sprinkled the wave image with lots of glitter, creating a glistening reminder of water flowing in the front door and imparting success.

2. Ring your doorbell daily! It calls the energy you desire into the home. Ring once for recognition, to be famous, and for positive attention. Ring twice for a lover or to attract any type of relationship. Ring three times for creative ideas and fertility and to bring children into the home. Ring four times for family harmony and to have the needed resources for the family and household expenses. Ring five times to call in spirit helpers, and that energy will also call in helpful people in real life. Ring six times to galvanize your career and call in success. Ring seven times to amplify learning and to be more knowledgeable. Ring eight times for more money and to build wealth. Ring nine times for all of these things at once—for glowing health, and happy surprises as well as overall good luck. Nine is the feng shui power number.

3. Make sure the path outside leading to the front door is clear and unimpeded. Sweep it periodically to keep the chi moving and fresh. Remove any weeds and make sure the shrubs and grass are well trimmed.

4. Clean the door. Hose it off outside and wipe it off on the inside. Use an abundance-oriented essential oil like spearmint in your wiping solution. You can mix the oil with hot water and some white vinegar.

5. Ensure the doorbell works! Let life signal you with good opportunities. And use the front door often to keep chi moving through this portal to your home.

6. Choose a welcome mat that invites good chi into the home. A plant or flower print is a symbol of living chi and will lend life to the space. One that depicts flowing water is always good, with bonus points if it looks as if it is directionally flowing into the home. Make sure the mat is fresh and clean and replace it when it is worn.

7. I learned a powerful technique from feng shui practitioner Karen Rauch Carter. She taught me to use a red spice like paprika or cinnamon and sprinkle it from the road all the way up to the front door and just over the threshold into the home. While you're scattering it, state your intentions. Think about what you want to draw into your life. This really works! It's an especially helpful technique if you have a long, winding driveway and cannot view the road from your front door. This helps the chi find its path in to bring you goodness.

8. The foyer is a great place for succulent plants because they hold water, which is the energetic equivalent of money and wealth. Put succulents by the front door to infuse their water energy into the career area and draw prosperity into the house.

9. Glass acts like water in the home and can add a sense of positivity, as well as fortune-building wealth chi. Water in the right places is very effective, but too much dampness where it doesn't belong can be destructive. Make sure that too much stagnant dampness doesn't accumulate in the foyer by gathering wet boots, shoes, and umbrellas in a container that is vented so they can dry out easily. Add glass decor that reminds you of flowing water, whether because of its shape, color, or other elements, because water symbolize even more money energy coming into your career sector. Most of these water and glass recommendations would also align well in the wealth corner of the bagua.

Refer back to The Elements section in the introduction and learn more about the front door as it relates to the bagua.

Vastu in the Foyer

We use Vastu to create a healing sanctuary in the home. Its impetus is that all spaces are sacred, and bringing that energy into the area of the front door sets the stage for a life of meaning and fulfillment.

Vastu Foyer Cures

Using some principles of Vastu in the foyer helps create a serene and plentiful space as you enter the home. Employing these strategies near the entrance invokes a sense of mindfulness in your house.

1. In the Vastu tradition, it is customary to remove your shoes upon entering the house, which is considered a sacred sanctuary to be revered and respected. And aside from spiritual considerations, a shoeless home is also better for hygiene and health.

2. Themes and patterns are an important element in the use of Vastu. One way to integrate a cohesive design sense that incorporates patterns is to choose one or two favorite colors and repeat them subtly through the home. Start in the foyer to set the stage and vibratory frequency for the repetition of colors and shapes you love, or overall thematic considerations like a repeating ikat print or subtle accents of zebra pattern. This will help you weave elements of your being into the home in a rhythmic way, diminishing tension and making you feel deeper comfort. One example would be to choose turquoise-colored accents in each room. These could be subtle, consisting of just a bit of the same color decorating a vase on the entryway table, the patterns on a pillow, the placemats in the dining room, and a toothbrush holder in the bathroom. Even when it's subtle, bringing the

FOYER

rhythm of a favorite color into your house can help give your space a sense of familiarity and make it more cozy and intimate.

3. In the same way, consider adding a design element or display pieces of a collection through the space. For example, if roses resonate with you, add fabric with variations of that pattern in different colors throughout several rooms, plus dried rose petal potpourri, and even rose essential oil diffused throughout the space to bring the energy of this symbol of harmony, love, and beauty into your home. You could begin in the foyer perhaps with a glass dish for keys to be stored that is patterned with roses and repeat a version of the design element throughout. It could also be a pop of velvet or linen in each room.

CHAKRA HEALING IN THE FOYER

Tapping into the power of your chakras to improve the energy of your front door area can bring a sense of groundedness to the home. It can help you feel present and in charge of your space, because you are fully infused in it.

Root Chakra

The root chakra is located at the base of your spine and governs your sense of security in the world. It is how and why you feel safe on an energetic and somatic level.

An incredibly important and practical concern for the front door and your overall feeling of security is to make sure it's always locked safely. That also means making sure the front door and all other doors and windows are secure and in good repair. We can implement all of the Vastu and feng shui cures in the world, but if you feel a sense of underlying stress about a broken latch on a window or even a shade that doesn't close all the way because it is broken, you still will feel off about your home. Safety first for a healthy and happy root chakra!

HOLISTIC HEALTH CHECK

Circulating fresh air in the home is a low-cost way to lessen the harmful effects of off-gassed chemicals that may be in the atmosphere. If you have a screen on your front door, consider opening it frequently to let the breezes blow in freely. Fresh air is your friend!

Root Chakra
Basic Trust

Sacral Chakra
Sexuality, Creativity

Solar Plexus
Wisdom, Power

Heart Chakra
Love, Healing

Throat Chakra
Communication

Third Eye
Awareness

Crown Chakra
Spirituality

WALLET
AND
PURSE MAGIC

ere are a few magical tips for adding a bit of luck and abundance to the place where you store your money. They have practical as well as energetic implications!

Clean out your wallet and purse and then add a pinch of salt to attract money. Ring a bell in or around your purse to activate the salt.

Organize your money and make sure all the bills are facing in the same direction. Order them from most to least and clean any receipts out of your wallet. Arrange your cards in an ordered manner, too.

Keep your purse off of the floor!

PART 2

REST & LOVE

In this section, we will explore the areas of your home in which you and your family rest, rejuvenate, and recharge. It's not just that we want to get enough sleep as well as a high quality of sleep in these areas—by employing the following techniques, you and your family will be able to be productive and live your best lives.

Because the security of slumber often dovetails with romance, we will also delve into love in all its forms. We will study how it manifests in our sleeping quarters and unlock the keys to intimacy, romance, passion, and amazing sex. We'll focus on ways to ignite your passions and increase your love while also balancing those fiery emotions with restorative periods of rest and rejuvenation.

CHAPTER 2

MAIN BEDROOM

*Y*our bedroom is one of the most important rooms of your home. You spend a significant amount of time there, and sleep is incredibly important to your health and well-being. Creating a bedroom that brings rest and passion to your life can be a true enhancement to your days and nights.

THE ENERGY OF THE BEDROOM

When we change the energy of the bedroom, amazing things can happen! My friend Karen Rauch Carter advises removing imagery of mermaids from the home and especially the bedroom. I know, mermaids are awesome. But they are depictions of single ladies, so if you want to be in a couple, they are sending the wrong message to life. Plus, they have no legs or feet and are therefore symbols of ungroundedness. So when I moved mine out to the patio, my love life flourished. I love mermaids, so I kept them, but they now frolic outside the house.

AROMATHERAPY FOR YOUR BEDROOM

Use the power of scent in the bedroom to encourage rest and serenity as well as stoke love, romance, and passion. For rest, lavender essential oil is the gold standard. For love, rose evokes affection in all of its forms—unconditional, romantic, universal. Jasmine is the best oil to

use for stoking passion. It activates kidney-channel yang from a Traditional Chinese Medicine perspective, and that is the energy of libido! Plus, it has an intoxicating fragrance. And for both relaxation and romance, ylang-ylang oil is a powerhouse.

It is a sedative and activates passion with its exotic scent. (Some plants contain multiple properties, sedative and aphrodisiac for example, which is relatively common in aromatherapy and herbalism.) You'll notice the difference in mood right away when you add the right scent.

DREAMY BEDROOM SPRITZ

Spray a few drops of this mixture on your linens to evoke beautiful dreams, rest, and romance. Because you will make this with organic, therapeutic-grade essential oils, you can also use it on your body as an intoxicating perfume!

Ingredients

Spring or distilled water to almost fill the bottle of your choice

10 drops of ylang-ylang essential oil

10 drops of jasmine essential oil

10 drops of Rose Otto or

Rose Absolute essential oil

Place all the ingredients into a clean spray bottle and mix well.
Shake each time before you use it.
You can spritz your sheets with the mixture
just before pulling up the covers.

Healing Power Mantras

My romantic relationship is beautiful, caring, passionate,
romantic, and enhances my life and my partner's life.
I sleep deeply and experience complete rejuvenation
and robust health from my time resting and sleeping in bed.
My bedroom brings me exactly what I need
for my very highest good.

MAIN BEDROOM

Houseplants for Your Bedroom

Houseplants are a delightful way to bring living chi or energy into your bedroom. They bring living chi to the sleep area and they also clean the air. If you choose to use artificial plants, be sure they are clean and in great shape.

Try an exotic Arabian jasmine plant in the main or master bedroom in your home. It will bring fragrance and living energy into the space. Jasmine is also an aphrodisiac that has sedative qualities, too, so it's a rare plant that

can help you accomplish both aims of this section: its fragrance can help you rest *and* enjoy romance.

Flowers are also always a good idea for the bedroom (provided you aren't allergic to their fragrance!). Consider adding a vase full of roses to the space. After all, roses are love embodied! And if you're looking for a color that will take it up a notch, there are a few options. Pink is a flirty, romantic color that will add joy and a lightly seductive energy to the bedroom. Red will light the match for a pop of fiery passion leading to enduring love. White brings serenity and restful purity. If you're looking for a more wide-ranging kind of creative passion, consider lavender roses, which are good for loving dreams, serenity, and can even support clairvoyance—the ability to see into the future—which is great if you're looking for insight on a future mate. Peach roses bring warmth and life to the room, so if you're trying to rekindle romantic flames, then they can be a good choice. Pale pink roses represent a calm and nurturing energy that can make partners feel safe and secure with each other. Bright yellow is a catalyst for communication and camaraderie. Pastel yellow soothes the soul and fosters balanced confidence.

CRYSTALS IN THE BEDROOM

Minerals in the bedroom can bring peace, calm, love, passion, and more. They are also beautiful, and the bedroom is an important place to include elements of beauty that delight the senses.

Use the following minerals to enhance the energy of the bedroom:

ROSE QUARTZ: Brings love in all forms! Use it liberally. Bonus: put it in groups of two in the bedroom to support good relationship vibes.

LARIMAR: A gorgeous stone infused with the essence of the blue ocean, some think its energy is aligned with the energy of dolphins. It infuses the bedroom with calm, serenity, and yin energy's nourishing essence.

PINK TOURMALINE: Pink tourmaline envelops lovers in a bedroom with sparkling romantic vibes. Love and appreciation abound when pink tourmaline is around. Swoon!

MOONSTONE: This gentle mineral brings yin essence and relaxes us to receive the bounty of deep rest.

SPIRIT HELPERS

To welcome the energy of the goddess into your bedroom for romance, consider invoking the Hindu goddess of love, Sati. She was the first wife of the Hindu deity Shiva. Together they are the embodiment of divine love. When Sati passed away, she reincarnated as the Hindu goddess Parvati and became Shiva's wife again. Their love was so strong that they magnetized each other through time and space multiple times.

Sati and Shiva's lovemaking was legendary and has connection to what we would refer to as Tantric philosophy and Tantric sex. It was not only about intoxicating passion and desire for these lovers, but also deep care, divine love, and emotional ecstasy that went hand in hand with the sensuous pleasure they shared. The energy of the goddess Sati can show you how to embody the divine feminine and her associated receptivity. Sati was also a fierce, cleansing goddess of rebirth and transformation. She can clear away the old and outdated using the fires of passion and desire and make way for new

heights of divine love and ecstasy available to you.

She is also known as an overarching feminine goddess who can assist not only with love and romance but also receive rest and restorative sleep.

Meditation to Invoke the Energy of Sati

State the following invocation aloud in the bedroom: "Dear Sati, please bring me divine love in my life and within myself. Let me experience boundless love, deep sleep, and rejuvenation with ease and grace."

Sati comes to you to help you let go of anything limiting your full enjoyment of the divine love coming your way. If you choose, tell Sati, "Yes," and she will clear you of old patterns. You can let go of learned behavior from the romantic relationships you witnessed as an impressionable child—for example your parents' relationship patterns. Commit to deep breathing as you let Sati help you. Bring your attention to the center of your chest and feel a pulsing or tingling there. Let go into it and relax your heart as you allow Sati to empower your heart center to receive the gifts of divine love. It is a fact that love is magnetized to you. That may be in a romantic form, but it may also appear in the love of friends, family, or community. Love is love and is beautiful between all genders or non-gendered folks, all sexual orientations, and more. Glory in that rush of feel-good chemicals and let it heal you. Let love help you become even more yourself.

Spirits of Place

Call in the spirits who govern the land over which your bedroom is built. Ask them for serenity and clear high-vibrational energy. State aloud in the bedroom, "I ask that all that transpires in this room be for the highest good of all life and in accordance with universal natural law, helping all, harming none. Please bring clear high-vibrational light into this space and clear the energy of this space to allow for deeply restful sleep filled with good dreams."

Animal Helpers

Connect with a guardian spirit or an animal helper for your bedroom. The loving, protective spirit of a whale or a panther is especially useful in this intimate space.

To invoke the whale, envision its presence outside the window ensuring cosmic dreams. For panther presence, visualize its spirit at the foot of the bed, guarding and protecting you. Allow the beautiful imaginative idea of an animal guardian to delight your imagination. You can say aloud, "I welcome the benevolent spirit of the panther and/or whale who is here to light up this room with good energy and peace. Thank you for your presence, dear friend."

Rose Love Ritual

Think about your intention for this ritual today. Is it infusing the room with unconditional love and self-acceptance? Or are you interested in amplifying the romance in your relationship? Do you desire more cuddling in the bedroom? Or more adventurous intimacy? Create an intention using affirmative statements. Here is an example: "This room is infused with romantic love and passion and each night restful sleep comes easily to all who sleep here."

Decide what color of rose—or multiple colors if you want multiple effects!—you would like to use for your ritual (see an overview of rose colors and their effects on pages 22–23). Next, find a beautiful way to display the roses that also conveys the intention you chose.

BURGUNDY: passion, desire

CHERRY RED: true love, lustful love

CLASSIC RED: romance, commitment to self-love and/or love of significant other

HOT PINK: flirtation, playfulness, sexy fun

MEDIUM PINK: mixing yin softness with lighthearted play, bliss

LIGHT PINK: nurturance, gentleness, soft, feminine yin

LILAC: spiritual opening to the sacred feminine, goddess energy

LAVENDER: money magic, wealth, mystical energy, enchantment

RICH PURPLE: royal queendom or kingdom of your
   life, luxury, opulence, spiritual opening
CORAL: energetic love, vital loving chi
SALMON: angels, enthusiasm for life, joy
PALE PEACH: restfulness, rejuvenation, relaxation,
   kinesthetic awareness
PEACH: gratitude for life, attracting blessings,
   opening the energy field to goodness
ORANGE: vitality, vibrant health, sensual vigor
YELLOW: happiness, gratitude for friendship, enacting
   your will in the world
CREAM: depth, introspection
WHITE: beauty, unity consciousness, clarity,
   channeling, spiritual sight

An example for the statement above might be to combine pink, red, and lavender roses in a smooth, sensually shaped bowl—maybe even heart shaped—with the roses trimmed short to float in clear, fresh spring water. As you prepare the roses and place them in your chosen vessel, state aloud the intention you created. Repeat it and feel its effects as if the intention already happened. Allow yourself to daydream in detail about what that would be like.

FENG SHUI IN THE BEDROOM

In feng shui, love and relationships are not associated with a particular element; however, it can be helpful to add a bit of fire to stoke the flames of passion and a *tiny* bit of metal for fertility and creativity. The metal can be useful if you are trying to conceive and also if you want to add more creativity to the romantic side of things in the bedroom or just to bring creative insights into your dreamtime.

The bedroom should be much more yin than yang. Think soft textures and fabrics, cozy warmth, and sensual elements that make the body feel good. Carpets and curtains that are soft, as opposed to hard floors and blinds, are yin-promoting and essential in the bedroom. Yin lighting is indirect. Warm light from dim lamps with rounded shapes and sumptuous fabrics add tenderness and the feminine energy necessary to receive pleasure and rest in the bedroom. Sleep is the ultimate yin activity!

Feng Shui Bedroom Cures

State aloud your intentions for the bedroom as you place some of the cures below. Pace yourself. You do not have to do them all at once.

1. **Pink is flirty and fun. Add it in abundance! All shades of pink make the bedroom romantic and restful all at the same time. Hot pink is sassy and super yin. Pale pink is relaxing and subtle and encourages restful sleep.**

2. **Red is fire. Heat things up with red to spice up the erotic side of life. Glazed tile and fired stone are fiery, so if you're decorating, consider integrating these materials.**

3. **Two is the number of romance. Pictures depicting pairs are great: for example, two love birds, two hearts, two flowers growing side by side. Or, add two natural beeswax candles**

scented with essential oils. Pop them in luxurious pink glass votives and display them in a pair. Two nightstands mean two people, so if you want a partner, make sure both sides of the bed have visually pleasing nightstands that are free of clutter. (Conversely, one means flying solo. If you're tired of the single life, take away any depictions of single people—single dancers, mermaids, knights, or whatever you're decorating with. Remove those!)

4. Fill the bedroom with life-supporting elements and eschew any dried flowers or dark imagery.

5. Remove mirrors from the bedroom—they're too yang—or cover them with a cloth every night. They make energy buzz around your room and interfere with your sleep.

6. Ideally, place your bed so you can see the door, and if you can, place the head of the bed in the north. If you can't place the bed so that its head is facing north, west or northwest will still contain your energy for better sleep. Plus, here's a bed-direction hack: head in north for more sex, west for more romance.

7. Wood is the best choice for the bedframe because it will not distort the sleeper's magnetic field. Wood is more yin and will attract more restful energy into your bedroom.

8. A solid headboard (not slatted) gives you support in an energetic sense. It has your back. Cover your headboard with fabrics to make it even more yin. Make the fabric luxurious to magnify the restful, relaxing, and romantic.

9. Keep laundry baskets that aren't being actively unloaded and any trash cans out of the bedroom. They hold dense energy that does not promote energy flow. Save them for other parts of the house that are better equipped to balance and withstand their chi.

Refer back to The Elements section in the introduction and find out where in the bagua your bedroom is located so you can apply additional cures to your room that might improve its energy even more.

VASTU IN THE BEDROOM

Vastu holds central the idea to create a sanctuary that is the home. This is especially important in the bedroom where you sleep. It is the perfect place to employ Vastu and create a spiritual sanctuary.

Vastu Bedroom Cures

Taking inspiration from the writings of Vastu, here are a few things you can do to improve the energy of your bedroom.

1. Keep adjoining bathroom doors, closet doors, and bureau drawers closed. Open doors and drawers invoke a feeling of clutter, which interferes with sleep.
2. Vastu wisdom suggests that you open the windows in the home daily including during winter even if only briefly to revitalize the home. It's also good for reducing VOCs!
3. Vastu suggests that sleep is deep spiritual surrender and so the room absolutely must feel like a secure, protective, comforting shelter. Think about what would inspire that feeling state for you. Maybe you have a little nagging question about the lock on the window in the back of your mind. Address it. Create a space that feels ultrasafe. Maybe keep a flashlight within reach under the bed in case the electricity goes out in the night.
4. Vedic wisdom asks us to make the main bedroom a romantic oasis through the use of beauty. Consider gorgeous expressions of intimacy and allure that touch your heart. What might delight you in your room? Perhaps you would enjoy fresh flowers, scents, or sumptuous art.

CHAKRA HEALING IN THE BEDROOM

There are several chakras that apply directly to the energies of the bedroom.

They are the sacral and heart chakras. Here are some tips for working with these chakras that will help you see immediate results.

Sacral Chakra

The sacral chakra is located in the lower abdomen, and is associated with creativity, sexuality, and reproduction. It opens you up to new experiences and encourages you to explore new possibilities.

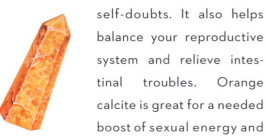

Orange calcite is a mood booster that interacts with your sacral chakra to alleviate depression and self-doubts. It also helps balance your reproductive system and relieve intestinal troubles. Orange calcite is great for a needed boost of sexual energy and can enhance a romantic evening by getting your sacral chakra spinning.

Often, our sexual freedom is blocked because we feel ashamed of our bodies' natural desires. A tea made from pine needles is just the thing to help cleanse you of any blame or regret you feel toward your own sexuality. Pine is often recommended for men who need a boost of testosterone, so a bit of pine's healing essence is ideal just before a romantic date night at home! You can diffuse a bit of pine essential oil in the bedroom or display some fresh pine boughs to enliven and heal sexual desire with a fiery burst of pungent pine.

Heart Chakra

The heart chakra is located in the center of your chest and is associated with compassion and love. When it is open, the heart chakra allows for you to express both self-love and love for others.

Known as the love stone, rose quartz opens your heart chakra and encourages unconditional love. It is a high-energy crystal and can enhance love and compassion in a variety of situations. Use rose quartz when you need a boost of self-love, or as a gift for

someone who you want to make sure recognizes the love you are feeling for them. Rose quartz is beautiful in jewelry, so it makes a great necklace that you can rest over your heart chakra to increase its effect.

Hawthorn berries strengthen your heart and your blood vessels. These delicious red fruits improve circulation but also heal at a meta-physical level. Hawthorn berries clear emotional blockages as they assist your heart physically, opening you up to experience joy and grati-tude. Hawthorn is also known to help begin the healing process if you feel your heart has been broken, so it is a great choice to bring to a friend getting over a breakup, or to take yourself when experiencing great loss. Hawthorn berries are beau-tiful when displayed fresh or dried and can be taken internally when correctly prepared. Create a beautiful display of berries in a flirty pink vase for health and playful fun.

BONUS CONTENT ALERT

Hop on to amyleighmercree.com/healinghomebookresources to get audio meditations to harmonize each of your chakras for use in specific rooms of the home.

Holistic Health Check

Do a quick sweep of the main bedroom and check for VOC-producing items like candles that are not made from beeswax. Pure soy wax candles do not release VOCs, but they do contribute to deforestation in many cases and are often grown with pesticides, so beeswax is the most environmentally friendly choice and is a bit healthier. Many candles are made from paraf-fin, which is a petroleum byproduct. Paraffin wax releases VOCs into the air when burned, so they should be avoided when possible.

TVs Are Rarely Sexy!

Keeping a television in the bedroom can sound cozy, but not only is it a great way to promote distractions that will inhibit you from connecting with your partner or centering yourself before bed, but if you tend to fall asleep to a flickering TV, its flashing light can also disrupt your rest. Use blue blocker glasses if you absolutely must have a television in your bedroom. But, word to the wise, televisions and other devices such as iPads, tablets, gaming devices, and phones are best left in another room while you drift off to sleep or spend intimate moments with your partner. These items are representative of the fire element in feng shui, which isn't especially beneficial to feelings of peace and security. They are beneficial in the fame and reputation gua, so move them there during the night and you'll feel the benefits!

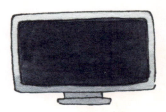

CHAPTER 3

Guest Room

*I*f you're lucky enough to have a special room just for guests, there are several ways in which you can direct the flow of energy to welcome them and make them feel appreciated and secure. Even if your guests are just crashing on your couch, there are still ways for you to produce the same effects!

The Energy of the Guest Room

As a highly sensitive person, I am selective about who I have in my home while I am sleeping. I feel people's energy—a *lot*. However, some of my best times with close friends happen when they come and stay with me. There is nothing like spending evenings talking and laughing in your pajamas and mornings having breakfast together.

Aromatherapy in the Guest Bedroom

Use scent in the guest bedroom to delight the senses and foster serenity. For rest, vetiver is wonderful! To bring harmony and agreeableness to your interactions with your honored guests, use wild orange oil.

WELCOMING GUEST BEDROOM SPRITZ

Use this easy linen spray to evoke sweet dreams. You can use it on bedroom linens or even suggest guests spritz it on their bodies.

Ingredients

Spring or distilled water to almost fill the bottle of your choice
10 drops of vetiver essential oil
10 drops of wild orange essential oil
(omit this if your guests get raines from oranges)
5 drops of sandalwood or rose absolute essential oil

Place all the ingredients in a clean spray bottle and mix well. Each time you use the spray, make sure to shake beforehand. You can spritz guest sheets with this mixture just before pulling up the covers.

HOUSEPLANTS FOR THE GUEST BEDROOM

The guest bedroom is a great candidate for easy-to-care-for plants since it is not used frequently. The common houseleek succulent will provide a soothing touch of calming beauty.

Tropical anthurium symbolizes hospitality and welcomes guests to your home. This flower can be used in an arrangement or as a houseplant.

CRYSTALS FOR THE GUEST BEDROOM

Sometimes a beautiful stone can bring a sense of peace to your guests and help them feel more secure while they are away from home.

Use the following minerals to enhance the energy of the guest room:

MOONSTONE: Brings yin energy and calms the spirit. It helps keep guests relaxed and nondisruptive.

CLEAR QUARTZ: This stone is centering and neutrally enlivening. It is good to smooth energy and is a great way to keep guests feeling like their visit is going well.

Spirit Helpers

To bring more harmony and good energy to the home while guests are staying over, call on the Greek goddess of home harmony, Hestia, to help your guests feel included and supported while they visit. As the goddess of the hearth, Hestia is associated with summer solstice and the warmth of fire.

Meditation to Invoke Hestia

State aloud the following invocation in the guest room: "Dear Hestia, please harmonize the energy of all of the inhabitants of this house, including any guests. Allow them to experience deep sleep and rejuvenation and stay for the perfect amount of time."

Hestia can help you today create a welcoming and relaxing environment in your home and she can bring the energy of harmony to your life. Just ask!

Healing Power Mantras

Honored guests sleep wonderfully in this room
and bring harmony and joy to this home.
This room attracts guests that I enjoy having in
my home in the quantity I desire.

Spirits of Place

Call in the spirits who govern the land over which your guest room is built. Ask them to clear the energy of your guests from the home after they leave. State aloud in the guest room after the guests leave, "I ask that all that transpires in this room be for the highest good of all life and in accordance with universal natural law, helping all, harming none. Please bring clear, high-vibrational light into this space and clear the energy of this room as needed."

Animal Helpers

If you'd like to help your guests have the best visit ever—and keep calm while entertaining others in your home—an animal helper can be hugely beneficial. A peacock is an excellent choice: elegant, assured, and calm. Envision a peacock made of light. You can picture its iridescent plumage glimmering in the room. Allow the beautiful idea of an animal guardian to delight your imagination. You can say aloud, "I welcome the benevolent spirit of the peacock who is here to light up this room with hospitality and beauty. Thank you for your presence, dear friend."

Epsom Salt Burning Ritual

The reason we include this ritual is that having a guest in the home, even a beloved one, can impact the energy of the house. In some cases, a little disruption can be positive and catalyzing. But even if it is, it is still a good idea to reclaim the energy of the home as your own and clear the density of other peoples' energy when they depart. You can also use this technique to clear your home after an illness, death, or when moving in to a new dwelling. Because this technique involves fire, please make sure you follow the safety precautions and never leave the fire unsupervised.

Materials

1 metal loaf pan
1 disposable aluminum roasting pan
Trivet or flame-resistant silicon mat
1/4 cup Epsom salts
3 tablespoons rubbing alcohol (91 percent isopropyl alcohol)
Long wooden match or long grill lighter

Instructions

Place the Epsom salt in the center of the loaf pan.
Pour the isopropyl alcohol over the salt, completely saturating it.

Place the trivet or silicon mat in the guest room. Put the roasting pan on top of it and the smaller loaf pan inside the larger pan, so you are using two metal pans and one is large enough to hold the other. This gives you two layers of safety and protection for this ritual. Keep it away from anything flammable, like fabric and carpeting. Ensure that there's an open area around the pan so it will not cause an unintended fire.

Say the following out loud: "I release all that does not serve me or the inhabitants of this house from this room for the very highest good of all life."

Light the salt and alcohol with the lighter or match. Be sure you keep your body and clothing far from the flame. Stand back and watch as the salt burns away completely. Make sure the pan is totally cool before you touch it or remove it. Do not leave the flames or embers unwatched and have a fire extinguisher handy for safety. After the ritual is complete, open the windows and doors and allow fresh, new energy to fill the space.

FENG SHUI FOR THE GUEST ROOM

The energy of the guest room should remain relatively neutral since different kinds of people will want to stay in it. Yin energy is conducive to sleep and rest, so you'll want to introduce soft fabrics and lighting to create a relaxing space for your guests. Unlike the main bedroom, you likely do not want to emphasize the sensual side of life, so focus on only soothing colors and decor. You can look at the bagua for the floor on which the bedroom is located and use pastel versions of the best colors for the area so you can maximize this relatively unused room's chi. Pastel colors will be more restful than bright vibrant colors, and we want to let your guests sleep deeply when they visit by creating a soft environment.

Feng Shui Cures for the Guest Room

Feng shui is a tool to increase the good energy of the home. Your guests will love it. The other people who will are those who live in the house. You will all feel better when the energy of the home is balanced and flowing.

1. Use a bell to easily remove the energy of guests after they leave. Ring it with the windows open and let the sound remove their energy.

2. To maximize abundance in the room, add a little bit of gold. This is a case where you can increase your prosperity by adding wealth energy to every room. That way, it infuses the whole house.

3. When the guest room is unused, make sure to periodically open the windows and turn on ceiling fans to keep its chi moving.

4. Round shapes are more yin and create effective communication, so use these elements in decorating the guest room so that you and your guests understand each other's needs and express them effectively.

5. Do not store too much excess clutter in the guest room. Clutter creates debt and dysfunction and is the enemy of wealth, so it's not a great idea to impose that weight on those who are visiting for just a short time. Open space lets in more abundance because there is room for it, so gift your guests with that energy.

6. If you must store something in the guest room, do it neatly. The least difficult things to store effectively, at least in an energetic sense, are soft, yin items like linens, towels, or out-of-season clothes.

7. Use a faceted feng shui crystal ball to keep the energy in this relatively unused room active and flowing. Add a red string to activate the chi even more.

8. In this bedroom, it also a good idea to have two nightstands and lamps to symbolize a harmonious relationship and push away the energy of going it alone. You want to convey that you and your guests are in it together!

9. To create a quiet and peaceful atmosphere to help guests relax at the end of a busy day, use cream colors to symbolize the north, night, and calmness. Use flowing glass shapes, perhaps cream-colored flowers in a curvy glass vase. To amplify harmonious energy, reduce the number of mirrors in this room.

> Refer back to The Elements section in the introduction and find out where in the bagua your guest room is located and apply those cures to the room.

Vastu in the Guest Room

Vastu places emphasis on serenity and the guest room is the perfect place to invoke tranquility and quiet restfulness.

Vastu Cures

Here are some cures that may help you improve the energy of your guest room. You can invite your guests to feel welcomed and appreciated with some of these cures, whether it is in a dedicated guest room or if they are sleeping in your living room for a few nights.

1. In Vastu, bringing nature into the home is recommended, and this free-flowing energy can be especially effective in the guest room. You can use plants, organic products, and things made from natural items like wood, dried flowers, and even essential oils to keep energy circulating.

2. Vastu wisdom suggests that you have guests sleep in the northwest of the home if possible, so they are enveloped with the element of air. This means that they will be less likely overstay their welcome.

3. Even the though the guest room is for guests, it should still feel connected to the rest of the home.

Remember to connect its decor and arrangement with your tastes. It's not a hotel!

Chakra Healing in the Guest Room

When guests visit, it is ideal for everyone in the house to be able to communicate clearly and with kindness. The throat chakra is the one to invigorate to accomplish this. Here's how!

Throat Chakra

The throat chakra is located at your neck and is associated with clear communication and expression. An open throat chakra promotes honesty and the ability to feel safe speaking your mind. It is a wonderful chakra to enhance in the guest room because it promotes clear communication in the home for all.

To open the throat chakra, whether your own or your guests', consider meditating with blue lace agate, a harmonious stone that enhances intuition and brings confidence. Associated with tact and clearness of expression, blue lace agate can help calm your nerves when speaking to guests you don't know well, ease the flow of a difficult conversation, and even assist with speech impediments and nervous vocal tics if your guests have them. It is a hopeful stone that encourages happiness and tranquility, so it is a great choice for balancing the throat chakra when you and your guests are struggling to communicate effectively.

Lemongrass is an excellent remedy for a sore throat and can be generally helpful for optimizing the energies of the throat chakra. It reduces inflammation and, as an herb of peace and healing, diffuses  anger, tension, and conflict. If a guest will be making a speech during his time staying with you (perhaps a wedding toast?), lemongrass

tea or a cocktail including lemongrass can be a great beverage to serve. And if things sour between you and your guests, it's great for calming them down and putting a stop to any escalating arguments. If guests are staying for dinner and you'd like to promote easy conversation, lemongrass is a great addition to soups or main courses. To help soothe a tense environment where the energies of the throat chakra are blocked, diffuse lemongrass essential oil through the guest room.

Holistic Health Check

Check the main guest room for stale air and off-gassing. Open the windows to clear the air daily. If you want to use air-freshening agents for this less trafficked room, remember to use pure essential oils. Peppermint and clove essential oils are natural bug repellents, so place a few drops in bedding to keep linens from getting stale and preventing any pests from accumulating there.

CHAPTER 4

CHILDREN'S BEDROOM

Your children's bedrooms are a place for them to rest and feel free to be themselves. They can feel peace and express themselves here without any judgment. Depending upon your children's ages, you may want to involve them in this process! You can determine what is age appropriate and let them help set the intention for their room with your guidance.

THE ENERGY OF A CHILD'S BEDROOM

A child's bedroom is a place for rest and rejuvenation. It is a sanctuary for the kid or kids who live there. Everyone needs a space to which they can go and be authentically and completely themselves, especially children.

AROMATHERAPY FOR A CHILD'S BEDROOM

To inspire relaxation and high-quality sleep in your child's bedroom, use the power of scent. To help your little ones drift into dreamtime with ease, use lavender and its mild, healing properties. To inspire imaginative time and to allow the nervous system to downgrade in a healthy manner, use neroli essential oil. A bedroom scented with neroli will promote the growth of a healthy imagination and help your child learn to self-soothe, so it's especially effective for anxious kids. Both lavender and neroli and their soothing qualities will also help with contentious siblings. Both inspire harmony and the open-mindedness required for listening.

SWEET DREAMS BEDROOM SPRITZ FOR KIDS

Use this easy linen spray for sweet dreams. Kids may enjoy helping you prepare this recipe, so feel free to involve them!

Ingredients

Spring or distilled water to almost fill the bottle of your choice

10 drops of lavender essential oil

10 drops of neroli essential oil

5 drops of rose otto or rose absolute essential oil

Place all the ingredients into a clean spray bottle and mix well. Shake each time before you use it. You can spritz the sheets with the mixture just before pulling up the covers.

HOUSEPLANTS FOR A CHILD'S BEDROOM

Try an indoor, potted orchid in your child's room. An orchid is an air plant, meaning in nature it sometimes grows above the ground in trees. Because it grows in exotic locations, it brings a sense of open skies and unlimited

Healing Power Mantras

Every child who sleeps in this room experiences deep,
restful sleep and feels refreshed and rejuvenated in the morning.
The children who inhabit this room enjoy being here,
feel relaxed and valued here, and can continue to
discover who they are and their hearts' desires in this space.

possibilities. It can inspire children to have beautiful dreams. Your children may enjoy having a spray bottle to spritz and water their orchid after you teach them about proper care of the plant. It is also a lovely opportunity to delve into the wonder of the botanical world with your kids.

If you'd like to add a flower arrangement to your child's room, try a colorful bouquet of gerbera daisies. They evoke cheerfulness and dispel bad feelings and the blues, which can help if your kiddo is going through a tough time. Kids can participate in the flower arranging and selection to take fun

ownership of their space and its energy. Just remember to keep any arrangements out of young children's reach, to prevent accidents!

CRYSTALS FOR A CHILD'S ROOM

By adding crystals to the decor of a child's room, you can help them regulate their emotions and have a happy day. Crystals can also improve the relationship between parent and child, or between siblings who might not always get along. Plus, what kid doesn't enjoy seeing a beautiful and sparkly stone on their shelf! Much like plants, having a crystal in the room is a great excuse to get your kids into the ins and outs of crystal healing. They might enjoy helping you pick out new additions once they familiarize themselves with the first ones you've added. Here are two to start:

SODALITE: This mineral is thought to promote clear thinking and light-heartedness, and inspire a sense of purpose. Sodalite promotes self-esteem and self-trust. It is also a very pretty bright-blue color, so children might enjoy having it around!

AMETHYST: This crystal imparts a sense of serenity and content-ment. It also facilitates a connec-tion to high-vibrational energy and gently promotes a healthy level of intuition. Amethyst helps create pleasant dreams,  and like sodalite, it's nice to look at: most amethyst is a brilliant shade of violet.

SPIRIT HELPERS

A child's room is a sanctuary from the outside world they are still learning about. It's important to invoke energies that help them feel supported so that when they venture out on their own, they can open themselves up to new opportuni-ties for growth. Artemis is the Greek goddess of independence and adven-ture. She is a patroness and protector of children, so it's a great idea to bring her energy into a child's room. She helps children feel a healthy sense of self-esteem and believe in their abili-ties. You can also ask this benevolent goddess to help dispel any nightmares with which your child may be struggling.

Meditation to Invoke the Energy of the Goddess Artemis

State the following invocation aloud in the children's room. If they are interested, you can invite them to say it with you, or instead of you. Say: "Dear Artemis, please fill this room with positive energy and impart a sense of healthy confidence and independence in the inhabitants. Allow them to experience deep sleep and reju-venation and have beautiful, comforting, and enjoyable dreams." If applicable, you can add, "Artemis please protect all who sleep in this room and bring only pleasant dreams. Thank you!"

Artemis will be thrilled to help enhance your children's lives. Her energy will give them an instant feeling of confidence.

Spirits of Place

Call in the spirits who govern the land over which your kids' room is built. Ask them to infuse the room with positive energy that inspires creativity in the daytime and relaxation and rest in the nighttime. You or your child can state the following aloud in the room: "I ask that all that transpires in this room be for the highest good of all life and in accordance with universal natural law, helping all, harming none. Please bring clear, high-vibrational light into this space and help create a beautiful life for its inhabitants."

Animal Helpers

You can invite your children to participate in this visualization if they are interested. When choosing an animal spirit to connect with your children's room, a dolphin is a good choice. The dolphin is an embodiment of happiness, bringing both security and jubilation into your children's lives. Dolphin energy ensures that your kids will wake up happy and excited to meet the day and go to sleep each night feeling gratified by their adventures.

Envision a playful dolphin made of light. It jumps and plays in your child's room, bringing delight. Allow the idea of an animal guardian to spark your imagination, and your children's imaginations if they are participating. You or your child, or both at the same time, can say aloud, "I welcome the benevolent spirit of the dancing dolphin who is here to light up this room with joy and rejuvenation. Thank you for your presence, dear friend."

MUGWORT SMOKE
SPRINKLE RITUAL

This mugwort smoke sprinkle is a form of smoke clearing. Smoke clearing is practiced all over the world in many cultures and in many different ways. In this case, you are mostly adding the energy of the mugwort plant to your space, as opposed to removing unwanted energy. In this ritual, you will be catalyzing the dried plant with the fire element and releasing it into the environment in a potent way. The energy of this plant is a great way to help your children sleep well at night. Mugwort is a botanical wonder. It promotes deep, pleasant, insightful dreams and is protective and purifying in nature—a great combination of properties to pass along to your kids. Again, this ritual involves fire, so take care to follow the safety precautions outlined below, and if children are participating, make sure they're supervised. Young children should not participate in this ritual.

CHILDREN'S BEDROOM

Materials

Heatproof bowl or dish
Dried mugwort (stalks or loose herbs)
Long wooden match or long grill lighter
Trivet or silicone mat, and/or thick pot holder or oven mitt

Instructions

You can do this with your children if they are interested.
Make sure to carefully monitor them if they assist you. Warn children of
the risk of fire and store all matches and lighters far away
from where their hands can reach them.

Place the mugwort in the bowl.

Place the trivet or silicone mat in the room. Put the bowl on top. Keep the bowl away from anything flammable like fabric and carpeting. Ensure there's an open area around the pan so it will not cause an unintended fire. Light the mugwort so that it emits a consistent stream of smoke. You may choose to carefully hold the bowl with the oven mitt and slowly move around the room, "sprinkling" the smoke throughout. Please be careful to avoid flammable surfaces and fabrics like curtains.

Say aloud: "I [or we if your child is there] allow pleasant, high-vibrational energy to fill this room with light and love for the very highest good of all life. That which is of the light fills this room." Waft the smoke through the room. Watch the mugwort burn completely, and when it is done, make sure the bowl and material are totally cool before touching them. Do not leave the flames or embers unwatched and have a fire extinguisher handy for safety. After the ritual is complete, open the windows and doors and allow even more fresh energy to fill the space.

Feng Shui for a Child's Room

The energy of children's rooms should promote sleep and rest but also be a place where children can express their individuality and interests and unleash their imaginations. A children's bedroom is their safe haven and sanctuary, so it should be protected when they are young, and as they get older, they can be involved in creating that environment as they develop their own tastes and preferences.

Yin energy is conducive to sleep and rest, so you should always try to use soft fabrics and lighting. This creates a relaxing space for your kids to unwind and let go of the focus they have to cultivate in school and life.

Feng Shui Cures for a Child's Bedroom

Here are a few things you can do to improve the energy of your children's bedroom with feng shui cures.

1. If children are sharing a room, help them define the space and boundaries of their individual and shared areas. Let them express their individuality by picking out bedding colors and patterns, as well as stuffed animals or decorations for their nightstands.

2. The direction the head faces during sleep influences sleep quality and brings all kinds of different chi to a child's life. This applies to children of all ages, including babies.

   a. When the bed faces east, it indicates growth energy, which is especially good for babies at the beginning of life. An eastern-facing bed also encourages brightness in the morning.

   b. When the bed faces southeast, it's conducive to sleep, growth, and development, as well as imagination and creativity.

   c. A southern-facing bed can result in poor sleep, but it does develop fast thinking and spontaneity.

LOVE &
LIGHT

d. A bed facing southwest produces a settled sleep, an abundance of caution, and the traits of caring and practicality.

e. Western-facing beds are great for kids who need a good quality of sleep, and this direction also leads to a playful, joyful spirit.

f. Northwest, on the other hand, indicates precocity and maturity—too serious for a baby! But maybe a good idea for an older child or a teen.

g. North is a good direction for a bed to face if your child needs direction or is having a challenge sleeping, but its positive effects are only good temporarily because the energy is too stagnant in the north for children over the long term.

h. Northeast causes tantrums and holds a hard energy, so if your child needs to be more competitive or has a contest or debate coming up, it can be a good temporary placement, but it is not generally advisable. And if you have a naturally combative child, you'll want to avoid it.

3. If you have the space in your house, it can be helpful to separate your child's playroom and bedroom. This creates a more settled energy. A room devoted exclusively to rest, if possible, can prevent conflict between the lively energies of a play area and the soothing energies surrounding the area where your child will sleep.

4. Bunkbeds are not ideal. Because one bed is over the other, this creates an overbearing energy in which the top bunk can dominate the bottom. This can incite conflict between children in bunk beds, so remove them if you can. If you can't, the dominant or older child should be given the bottom bunk to balance the dynamic between top and bottom. Be sure to have the child who sleeps in the bottom bunk decorate

the underside of the bed above. Help them expand into that space and claim it as their own. If the beds are detachable, move one end of the bed out from under the bottom bunk at a right angle to gain more spaciousness. For all bedrooms including your children's, all beds should be placed so that there is a wall behind the head side. This creates the feeling that life "has your back."

5. If your child is drawn to animal prints or decorations, let them use those adornments in their room. This helps your child claim their autonomy and feel empowered. These items bring a little fire energy into the space, which is catalyzing and creates good luck.

6. All bedrooms relate to relationships, so encourage children to display a few fun pictures of family and friends who make them feel loved and accepted to bring that supportive energy to the room.

7. Bright colors are generally a bit more on the yang side. Steer children toward softer versions of their favorites for bedroom decor so they have a good balance of playful and restful energy. So, instead of crimson red, consider a more muted coral or rust. Instead of bright orange, try peach—and so on.

8. If your children have a desk in their room, make sure it is kid size so they feel confident, balanced, and able as opposed to feeling too small. If they are swimming in an adult-size desk, they will feel unable to achieve challenging goals. (If possible, an even better alternative is to put the desk in another quiet room, so any homework stress isn't near the child during rest time.)

9. Help children pick a dedicated spot to display awards, trophies, good grades, artwork, and things that inspire them to feel proud. Imagine the bagua over the child's room. The fame and reputation area will be straight back from the door where you enter, all the way at the back of the room. If possible, place these items near that area.

VASTU IN A CHILD'S ROOM

Vastu aims to create a complete sanctuary in the home. This intention is especially fitting for a child's room. When kids feel in tune with their rooms and have an appropriate sense of ownership, meaning they see their tastes reflected there, they have a place where they can be themselves without judgment.

> Refer back to The Elements section in the introduction. Find out where in the bagua your children's room is located and *gently* apply those cures to the room. Go easy so as not to overwhelm your child energetically.

1. Be sure to have a nice place for your children to keep their books. And make sure your child has paper books, as opposed to ebooks on an iPad or other device. Printed books make the pursuit of knowledge alluring and will promote a love of learning.

2. Vastu wisdom suggests that each room have a "zone of tranquility," which is an area to quietly read, relax, and in some cases meditate. Placing this area in the east or northeast will help calm rowdy children.

3. In Vastu, your children's bedroom is meant to nurture mind, soul, and self-esteem. It is a place that helps your children feel loveable and worthy. Invite your children to add some favorite design element to their room while preserving a sense of tranquility. Perhaps an image of a favorite animal, mythical creature, type of car, construction equipment, or favorite color. This lets your children feel like their interests are accepted and they are validated. They can feel secure and relaxed in their own space.

CHAKRA HEALING IN A CHILD'S ROOM

Using chakra healing in your child's room can promote overall well-being and harmony. It is a way to increase their happiness and bring balance to their room.

Heart Chakra

The heart chakra is located in the center of the chest and is associated with compassion and love. It is incredibly important for children to feel loved. This foundation is a critical key to the sense of self and belonging every child requires.

To open the heart chakra, focus on remedies that make children feel supported and secure. Amber is a gold-colored fossilized resin that promotes these energies. Children are attracted to this gentle substance. Some people place amber chip necklaces on teething toddlers to help soothe them during this painful period. Amber emits a sunny and calming energy, so it is also a great item to have present in birthing rooms.

Chamomile is an excellent plant for children that can also balance the heart chakra. It calms the nervous system and promotes relaxation. It has a gentle and appealing scent and taste. Chamomile herbal infusion (commonly but incorrectly referred to as herbal tea) is safe for children of all ages. Chamomile flowers are also lovely when displayed, and chamomile essential oil can be diffused in a child's room to create an inviting energy for sleep and rest. Olfactory beauty is in the eye of the beholder, or in this case the smeller, so it is important that your child likes the scent. You can diffuse it with some sweet orange oil if you'd like to add sweetness. Please note: some people who are prone to migraines are triggered by consumption of oranges and may experience the same result with the essential oil, so keep that in mind if you're adding orange oil.

HOLISTIC HEALTH CHECK

Check your children's room for toxic hazards. First, check the fabric content of all of the fabrics in the room, including cushions, carpets, clothing, bedding, and curtains. Pure cotton or linen

Eschew pieces of furniture made from veneered wood (chemically treated) and MDF (medium-density fiberboard); the latter is thought to off-gas formaldehyde. When possible, opt for wood that is not pretreated with chemicals for furniture and avoid plastics in general. That includes toys. Try to choose natural fiber toys like those made from wood or cotton as opposed to plastics and synthetic-fiber toys that are often treated with carcinogenic flame retardants.

You might also consider encouraging children to care about the planet by explaining how their toys are made, and why you've picked certain products for your home and avoided others. Involve your children in making your home more environmentally friendly by learning more about protecting the planet together: research how products are made, whether that process is good for the environment, and whether that item is healthy for human bodies.

are natural fibers that are kind to your children's skin, as well as the environment. It's especially import-ant to make sure pajamas, sheets, underclothes, and fabrics closest to children's skin are free of synthetic fibers that may have negative health effects. The process of creating poly-ester creates toxic by-products that are harmful to the environment, but it's also not an absorbent material, which can promote the growth of unhealthy bacteria.

A Word About Screens

Devices in any bedroom are clinically proven to interrupt sleep. Stow them outside of the sleeping area and opt for books and printed reading materials. For kids, if they are permitted to game on devices, it's better to store them outside the bedroom so no one is tempted to take up gaming in the middle of the night, and their energy is far away from sleeping kids.

PART 3

NOURISHMENT & LIVING

*I*n this section, we will explore the areas of your home in which you and your family nourish yourselves through meals, time spent together, and leisure time. In your kitchen and dining room, you prepare and consume food and beverages. They are converted into energy that helps you power your day, so the chi in these rooms can add more good fuel to your storehouse if it is properly cultivated.

In this section, we will also explore the rooms where you spend time transitioning from work to rest. The living room and den are frequently used rooms where we unwind and shift gears. All of those rooms are places where family members and housemates gather, and so they are places where we derive feelings of support and belonging.

CHAPTER 5

KITCHEN

The kitchen is a place for warmth and gathering in many households. It is where we gather nourishment and receive nurturance. We prepare food there, which is incredibly important because it is how we fuel ourselves. So maximizing healing chi in the kitchen is very important.

THE ENERGY OF THE KITCHEN

The power of the kitchen in the home is vast. I had a client a few years back who received a moderate medical diagnosis that required a lifestyle change to overcome. She chose to overhaul the energy of her kitchen while also upgrading her diet. She switched to mostly organic foods at home and eliminated most plastics from the kitchen. At the same time, she added therapeutic-grade, organic essential oil aromatherapy elements and health-promoting houseplants. Plus, she invoked several helpful goddess spirits for her health and home. Eight months later, her health had drastically improved, and she reported feeling more balanced and joyful in her life.

AROMATHERAPY

Scent in the kitchen can stimulate appetite for healthy foods and lively conversation as well as mindful eating. Tangerine essential oil can be diffused

KITCHEN

or simmered on the stove to help family members who might need encouragement to be nourished by food—it's a great appetite stimulant. Spearmint has a similar effect and pairs well with tangerine. Try grapefruit oil in the kitchen in the morning to start the day on a cheerful note and clove on a cold winter's eve (it's also wonderful for immunity and cold prevention).

KITCHEN SOCIAL SPRITZ

Use this easy aromatherapy spray to create a pleasant atmosphere for family meals or to socialize. You can also diffuse this blend or simmer it on the stove. Use it on your body as a warming perfume. You can also use it to wipe down counters and surfaces, and it's good for deodorizing. Clove is antibacterial, antiviral, and antifungal, and sweet orange is also antibacterial.

Ingredients

Spring or distilled water to almost fill the bottle of your choice

10 drops of sweet orange essential oil
10 drops of clove essential oil
10 drops of fennel essential oil

Place all the ingredients into a clean spray bottle and mix well.
Shake each time before you use it.
You can spritz tablecloths, surfaces, linen napkins,
and the corners and center of the room.

Houseplants for the Kitchen

We can use houseplants to bring life and abundance into the kitchen. It's not just that it's pleasant to see a bit of greenery in the place where the freshness of ingredients and their effect on your health is so important. The energies of particular plants are often perfect for stimulating appetite, assisting mindful cooking, and making food taste great. In the kitchen, make meals dynamic and memorable with the unconventional energy of red desert gem cacti. They are unique and bold alternatives to the standard mini cactus, adding liveliness to the kitchen with a bright splash of color.

To bring chi into the room, consider sweet basil. Sweet basil flowers create good fortune, and the herb basil also brings prosperity. You can display the flowers in a vase or place a basil plant in the kitchen so that you can use some of the leaves for cooking when needed. If you let your basil grow all the way to the flowering stage, you can choose to enjoy the flowers or add them to your cooking,

Healing Power Mantras

This kitchen brings nourishment, contentment, and joy to all who enter.
The inhabitants of this home receive high-vibrational fuel and energy with the help of this healthful kitchen, and quality of life is enhanced for all who enter.
This kitchen is supercharged with health-giving, high-vibrational frequencies that are transmitted though eating and preparing food and beverages here.

KITCHEN

savoring their delightful scent, texture, and color in addition to flavor.

CRYSTALS IN THE KITCHEN

To enhance the energy of the kitchen, consider minerals that stimulate conviviality and health.

TOPAZ: This mineral is known as the stone of success and true love. It promotes individuality and creativity and instills confidence. It replaces negative energy with joy and cheer. It's perfect for communal rooms like the kitchen.

SUNSTONE: This stone promotes creativity and good luck! It alleviates stress and increases vitality. It brings people together while simultaneously cleaning their chakras and infusing them with positive energy.

CLEANING YOUR CRYSTAL HELPERS

It is necessary to cleanse the crystals in the home frequently. The clearer they are, the more they can enhance the energy of the home.

Here are ways to cleanse your crystals:

RUNNING WATER: Allow the crystals to be submerged and feel the old, dense energy being washed out of them and down the drain. When the crystals are clean, set them out in direct sunlight so that they can dry naturally. Note that this technique should not be used for crystals that do not do well in water, like opals and sapphires.

SUN AND MOONLIGHT CLEANSING: Crystals prefer to be outside, exposed to light and moisture, and ideally on the ground. Place them outdoors or in the garden frequently and for long periods of time.

SALT, EARTH, OR SAND CLEANSING: Place the crystals in a bowl of salt, clean dirt, or sand: use plain, untreated sea salt. Let them sit for at least twenty-four hours. You can leave them even longer, even months or years! They love this method. Then remove them and feel their clean, unblocked energies flowing.

Spirit Helpers in the Kitchen

The ideal image of a kitchen is one in which this room is the site of a never-ending feast, full of delicious food and great conversation. The Mid-Autumn Moon Festival is an auspicious occasion celebrating the fullness of the moon and marked by the consumption of delicious food, including the mooncake. To call upon the happiness of reunion, completion, and celebration, consider bringing the energy of the Taoist goddess of the moon, Chang'e, into your kitchen. She is a much-revered goddess venerated during the Mid-Autumn Moon Festival. Chang'e is a powerful yet nurturing queen of the moon who lives there with her jade rabbit and jade dragon. On the night of the autumn full moon, people eat mooncakes in her honor.

Chang'e is a force of nourishing balance and yin power. Her feminine energy can bring harmony, balance, and equanimity to the kitchen. Chang'e's essence also can infuse the food prepared in the kitchen with positive energy. She is symbol of symbiotic balance, which occurs between any two living things when their mutually beneficial relationship creates balance for both of them. The moon and the earth are in symbiotic balance via their gravitational relationship, and in the same way, Chang'e can help bring that useful energy to your life and home.

Meditation to Invoke the Energy of Chang'e

To invoke the symbiosis of the sun and moon embodied by the energy of Chang'e, look at the moon and feel yourself communing and communicating with it, either silently or aloud. Feel the moon. Speak to it and receive its messages of healing light and loving support. Do this often. Its abundance

is being offered. Imagine what kind of conversation you might have with the moon. What would you ask about? What might be the answer? Try it.

Say the following affirmation aloud: "I exist in symbiotic balance with all life for all time. Each and every moment of my life is mutually beneficial for me and whomever or whatever I encounter. I am deeply, truly balanced and well. I *am* balance. My balanced self resonates through my home, and all who are present here exist in balance when in these walls."

Spirits of Place

Invoke the spirits who are responsible for the land over which your kitchen is built. Ask them for harmony and high-vibrational joy. State aloud in the kitchen, "I ask that all that transpires in this room be for the highest good of all life and in accordance with universal natural law, helping all, harming none. Please bring harmonious light into this space and clear the energy of this space to allow for nourishing food to be prepared and joyful conversations and camaraderie to occur."

Animal Helpers

The kitchen is the perfect place for the animal spirit of the monkey. Monkeys are very social animals and are playful and fun. This is wonderful energy to bring into the kitchen. The kitchen can be a place of lively, harmonious conversation, and the monkey's energy of easy communication helps so much. Allow the idea of an animal guardian to enchant your curiosity. The energy of the monkey invokes a spirit of gregarious joy and agreeableness. You can say aloud, "I welcome the playful spirit of the monkey to enliven this kitchen with nourishment and happiness. Thank you for your presence, dear friend."

PROSPERITY DINNER RITUAL

Do this ritual as you are preparing a delicious, high-quality meal. You can do this alone or with your dinner companions. Whether solitary or communal, the steps of this ritual will infuse the meal with the energies of prosperity and abundance using the power of intention. As you place your attention on prosperity, you will begin to think in terms of it more.

Set an intention prior to preparing the meal using an affirmative statement. Try something like, "My life and home are prosperous, and wealth and money flow to me easily and effortlessly. The meal I am about to create is a symbol of the luxurious good life. I honor, love, and deserve money and wealth and will use it for my good and the good of others. Please infuse my being with prosperity for all time."

Gather the ingredients for the meal. Choose high-quality supplies for this ritual meal, including organically grown food if you can get it. This is a great time to include special ingredients that will make the meal feel special and exciting.

As you lay out the ingredients, repeat aloud, "I love money, and money loves me." Sing a favorite song and feel joy. Light a candle and reflect on your shining light from within. Reflect on all of the love and abundance you share and experience. Feel gratitude. You are so abundant. You are in your home, preparing a lovely meal. You have so much. Breathe into the center of your chest and feel

KITCHEN

gratitude. List ten things, situations, or experiences for which you are grateful—this can be a mental list or you can use this as an opportunity for a gratitude activity with your dinner companions.

Cook and feel the warmth of the stove, the hearth, which is a symbol of plenty and comfort. As you create the meal, feel the gratefulness and repeat affirmative statements of joy, abundance, and prosperity. Say things like:

I am joy.

I am filled with gratitude.

My life is beautiful.

Money is my good friend.

My life is rich and plentiful.

I feel fulfilled and content.

When the meal is ready, serve it with gorgeous cloth napkins, your best dishes, and candles on the table. Add some flowers for decor and even organic edible flowers to garnish if you can find them. As you enjoy the meal, feel the abundance and fortune of your life and being. Enjoy and affirm it and allow it to proliferate.

Feng Shui in the Kitchen

The kitchen is a smart place to include yang elements. Yang energy feels orderly and functional. It allows us to create structure in our lives and yang also fuels dynamic action.

Shiny, flat surfaces speed up the flow of chi and make it more yang and active. These surfaces are perfect for the kitchen. Direct lighting is also more yang. In the kitchen, it is also functional because we need to be able to see well when we are chopping vegetables and cooking, using a hot stove. Strong lines and defined shapes create a more yang atmosphere as well.

However, for balance, it is advisable to have a bit of yin to balance the yang in any room. Yin is health promoting in many ways that are often lacking in our fast-paced society—yin is rest, relaxation, formless thoughts, an antidote to the "go, go, go." Sleep is the ultimate yin activity. And rest is a close second. So it is always important to make sure a least a bit

of yin is represented. The yin in the kitchen is the warmth of cooking and camaraderie. It is the towels, the cloth napkins, the fabric placemats. Natural fibers better encourage the flow of chi, so prioritize fabric over plastic.

The fire element is very important in this space as it is synonymous with the hearth. The hearth is one of the most important features in the home and, in this case, it is represented quite literally as the stove. Keep it clean!

Feng Shui in the Kitchen Cures

State your intentions for the kitchen aloud as you place some of the cures below. Pace yourself. You do not have to do them all at once.

1. **Envision the bagua overlaid on top of the stove's surface. So the career area is at the front and center of the stove, and so on. Cooking on the burners in each area brings dynamic and warming hearth energy to that area of your life, enlivening it. Use all of the burners relatively equally**

to keep the chi in your life evenly distributed and flowing well.

2. Use symbols of the earth element to feed fire and stabilize the energy of the room. Add clay pottery, square items, and yellow and earth tones.

3. The food you eat will be stored in your kitchen or pantry, and the chi of the room will influence that food. Keep the kitchen free of dampness to avoid stagnation in your kitchen chi and the energy of your body. Use exhaust fans and open windows as needed.

4. It is important to allow your kitchen to be filled with natural light. It is nature's light and therefore full of chi energy, which will fuel you and your family. So open blinds and curtains and let there be light.

5. Natural materials are excellent in the home and particularly in the kitchen. Wood promotes a natural feeling and a slightly more yin energy. Stone will generate a more yang energy. Both are good in the kitchen! So, notice what you feel drawn to.

6. Synthetic materials block the flow of chi and are best avoided. Take a look around the kitchen and see if there are any synthetics you could replace with natural materials.

7. Healthy plants foster healthy chi! They also absorb moisture from the air, helping rid the kitchen of dampness. In Traditional Chinese Medicine, dampness or damp accumulation is a cause of certain health ailments. So healthy hydration is great, but dampness in the home where it doesn't belong is not ideal.

8. Soft white and incandescent lighting, as opposed to fluorescent lighting, will limit your exposure to electromagnetic radiation. Dimmer switches and different lighting options can give you lots of choice to vary lighting as desired.

9. Keep surfaces clutter free and ensure that everything has a place so the chi of the room can move easily and freely. Invest in smart storage and take the time to keep the area organized.

KITCHEN

Refer back to The Elements section in the introduction to find out where in the bagua your kitchen is located and apply those cures to your room, too.

VASTU IN THE KITCHEN

The writings of Vastu include insight on kitchens and other places where food is prepared and consumed. The energy of food and beverages are enhanced by focusing on the chi via mindfulness and singing the Vastu idea of home as sanctuary. So assembling meals in a sanctuary of good energy enhances the quality of your life.

Vastu Kitchen Cures Here are some cures that may help you improve the energy of your kitchen. You can invite your guests to feel welcomed and appreciated with some of these cures.

1. In the Vastu tradition, sunlight should shine on a kitchen, ideally during the day when food is being prepared. Facing east while cooking or assembling food will also infuse your meals with symbolic sun energy, which in turn will infuse the food with life force. The sun deity, Surya, is considered the sustainer of life, and that energy will enliven food prepared in this manner.

2. The Vastu zone of tranquility in the kitchen can be well placed by putting a symbol of a favorite deity over the kitchen sink so that you see it frequently. When you are enacting a rhythmic and repetitive task like chopping veggies or washing dishes, you can allow your mind to gently contemplate the image and allow it to energize you.

3. Spices enliven and give life. Keep them colorfully displayed as functional decor. You can also grow fresh herbs on a sunlit windowsill to bring life, light, and flavor to the room.

4. Vedic wisdom favors gentle and nurturing colors as well as simple and
functional objects without extra-
neous items that are not for the
kitchen, so keep items that aren't
necessary for kitchen activities out
of this room!

Chakra Healing in the Kitchen

We can connect with the energy of the chakra system to make the kitchen an oasis of good health and vitality. In the section below we will strengthen the chi of the chakra that can help in the kitchen.

Solar Plexus Chakra

The solar plexus chakra is located by your breastbone and is associated with self-confidence and strength. It stimulates happiness and power and, when blocked, can lead to your being overly judgmental. Because the kitchen should be a welcoming space where all are nourished, this tendency can keep it from being the hub of your home.

Often called the stone of abundance, citrine is a wonderful choice to heal your solar plexus chakra and increase your self-esteem to prevent these tendencies. It promotes success and mental clarity and can magnify your personal power and energy. Citrine fights against negative energies, so it is a great choice to use when you want to cleanse your home or work environment. It clears negative energies without absorbing them. Just pop it on the windowsill periodically and let sunlight energetically rinse it.

Marshmallow leaf is best known for its initial involvement in the manufacturing of marshmallows, but as an herb, it makes a soothing, comforting tea that balances your solar plexus chakra. It helps with digestion, and reconnects you to your breath, helping you relax and embrace your natural confidence. It is yin promoting and nourishing to kidney chi. It is good for almost all constitutions.

HOLISTIC HEALTH CHECK

You may have heard of the benefits of organic food, but if you are making over the energetic properties of your kitchen, you have even more of a reason to consider adding them to your diet. There are plenty of reasons to eat organically grown food that is free of pesticides and farmed using environmentally sustainable methods, but suffice it to say that organic foods are a great way to nourish your family and, in doing so, increase the healing energies in your home.

You have the power to affect environmental change on our planet by choosing to purchase organic fruits, vegetables, and other foods. You can be a force in preventing soil and underground water contamination caused by conventional farming, which uses large quantities of artificial fertilizers and pesticides, many of which have been proven to be carcinogenic. Organic farming is also better for local wildlife. By not poisoning the natural habitat for plants with toxic chemicals, a kinder and less impactful farmer reduces the harm caused to local flora and fauna. Organic farming also helps fight global warming by producing fewer greenhouse gases and encourages biodiversity. Biodiversity encourages the balance of nature and keeps more species of plants and animals happy and healthy. It is the way Mother Nature intended flora and fauna to live together. We are fauna. We are animals. Human animals. We have the opportunity to make a positive difference on our planet by choosing to put our money into causes in which we believe. By purchasing organic foods, we promote a kinder and gentler planet.

CHAPTER 6

DINING ROOM

The dining room can be a casual place of gathering and warmth and an elegant place for gracious dinners and larger parties. Either way, we can influence the energy of the area so that we experience our best outcomes.

THE ENERGY OF THE DINING ROOM

Your favorite holiday has arrived. You shop for decorations and the most delectable foods. You gather family and friends and host a dinner in your dining room. The energy there is flowing and free, so the conversation is, too. Warm votive lights send the glow of candle-light throughout the room. Your guests are bathed in a cozy glow, smiling and enjoying the delicious treats. This can be you, once you renovate the energy of this space. Read on to find out how.

AROMATHERAPY FOR THE DINING ROOM

Use aromatherapy in the dining room to enliven the space and create a convivial atmosphere. Clean, stimulating scents can create a sense of vibrancy and togeth-erness. Use coriander essential oil to stimulate lively conversation and create a warm atmosphere. Add the scent of lemongrass to invigorate the energy of the room.

DINING ROOM DYNAMIC SPRITZ

Use this easy aromatherapy spray to create a pleasant atmosphere for family meals or to socialize. You can also diffuse it or simmer it on the stove, or even use it as a perfume while hosting the dinner party of your dreams.

Ingredients

Spring or distilled water to almost fill the bottle of your choice

10 drops of lemon essential oil
10 drops of clary sage essential oil
10 drops of grapefruit essential oil

Place all the ingredients into a clean spray bottle and mix well. Each time you use this spritz, make sure to shake beforehand. You can spritz tablecloths, surfaces, and linen napkins. Make sure to give corners a spray, as well as the center of the room.

HOUSEPLANTS FOR THE DINING ROOM

A ginger plant is a great way to get dinner guests in the dining room to open up and start a lively conversation. Ginger brings warm, novel energy into the space to allow your guests to relax and feel comfortable expressing themselves. Place your ginger in a warm spot in the room and keep it nicely spritzed with water to simulate its native environment in tropical and subtropical regions, which is naturally warm and humid. You can teach children to spritz the ginger plant, too, since it is hardy. It is a plant that is used to receiving partial, not full, sunlight so it will thrive indoors as long as it is kept near a window.

Birds of paradise flowers create thoughtfulness, which is another property that is helpful to add to a meal. Caring and love can keep family and friends eating dinner together, appreciative and open to hearing what one another has to say—and this energy has the added benefit of staving off arguments. Birds of paradise flowers can also bring the energy of fidelity and loyalty to your space, reminding everyone around the table that they are all together and should be thankful. This is a wonderful flower to display in the dining area. It can vivify the room with its color and texture. The novelty of this plant also brings interest and nonconformist thinking—not a bad thing to have at a fun dinner party!

CRYSTAL IN THE DINING ROOM

Crystals are a beautiful addition to a dining room centerpiece or along a sideboard as a decorative accent, but they are also vessels for energy that can be helpful in keeping a meal civil, spicing up dinner

Healing Power Mantras

Everyone who dines here is nourished with healthy fuel and positive energy.
This room is a place of joy, happiness, and serenity.
When one is dining in solitude here, mindful eating and deep rejuvenation occur.
When a group dines here, the conversation is lively, caring, respectful, and harmonious. Everyone has a positive experience and feels a pleasant sense of belonging.

party conversation, or simply adding an element of stability to a place where friends and family gather.

CITRINE: This mineral is a type of quartz. It brings vitality and life to an area. It also clears the room gently and easily like a ray of sunlight. It balances yang and yin and attracts and maintains wealth and prosperity. It is good for many rooms, but particularly the dining room, which is functionally the seat of many gatherings.

FLUORITE: This stone creates strength and order. It stabilizes chaos. Fluorite helps relationships to flourish and finds the highest outcome for the group. It

promotes good health and purification and allows us to absorb yin energy—so it's perfect for a meal among people who love one another and need a moment of Zen.

SPIRIT HELPERS IN THE DINING ROOM

The dining room can be the focal point of a party, where everyone sits down for a celebratory meal. That means invoking the energy of a deity who is often known as the life of a party, the bringer of good fortune and celebration, as well as a fixer of problems. Ganesha, a Hindu deity, serves as a spirit guide for many people all over the world and is very much beloved as an expert at helping us overcome obstacles. Legend has it that he has a loving pet in the form of a mouse who chews right through anything that gets in the way of his charges' highest good.

Ganesha is a lover of the good life and helps you experience luxury and that which makes you feel good in healthful manner. He can ignite the sensual if it is a romantic dinner. Or he can infuse the space with positive energy and remove negativity if the whole family is gathering, so the meal can be happy and pleasurable for all.

Ganesha is also known as a creative being who inspires. So he can bring fresh perspectives, new ideas, and artistic inspiration. This can be useful as you are working things out in conversation or if you are doing a craft or creative project in the dining room between mealtimes.

Meditation for Invoking the Energy of Ganesha

Say the following affirmation aloud: "I invoke the delightful power and pleasantness of Ganesha to elevate the frequency of this space. I allow this room to become a haven of good fortune and creative inspiration. All that occurs here and in this home is watched over by Ganesha and for the highest good of all life, helping all and harming none. I allow Ganesha to fill the lives of the inhabitants of this house with wealth and prosperity. It is done."

Spirits of Place

Commune with the spirits who are responsible for the land over which your dining room or dining area is built. Ask these beings for joy and high-vibrational creative harmony. State aloud in the dining room, "I ask that all that transpires in this room be for the highest good of all life and in accordance with universal natural law, helping all, harming none. Please bring joy into this space and enliven it with light and happy energy to allow for nourishing food to be consumed and harmonious times to be had by all who enter."

Animal Helpers

The dining room is the perfect place for the fiery animal spirit of the mythical dragon. Fire energy is called for in the dining room to stoke the joyful flames of camaraderie and communal enjoyment of food. The dragon also offers an element of wisdom. Allow the exciting concept of an animal guardian to pique your interest. Think of the internal warmth a dragon holds. Its benevolent nature means it keeps you warm and helps you fly to the heights of which you dream. You can say aloud, "I welcome the healthy fire of the dragon to warm and illuminate this dining area with love and joy. Thank you for your presence, dear friend."

DINING ROOM

CLEARING MEAL PREPARATION RITUAL

Enact this ritual prior to eating a meal in the room. You do not have to do it every time you eat in there, but if you aim for once per week, it will help keep the energy of the space fresh and light. This ritual will prevent arguments and disagreements and generally provide a friendly, blank slate for all the gatherings that will happen there.

Open all windows if you can. Prepare a bucket or bowl of hot tap water. Add a few tablespoons of finely ground sea salt. Or you can add an essential oil or two if you'd like—I recommend lemon, thyme, or clary sage, but any oil that you enjoy will be lovely.

Using a clean kitchen towel, dip it in the mixture and wring it out. Use the towel to give all surfaces a salty, clearing wipe down. Repeat, dipping, wringing, and wiping until all surfaces have been cleaned. This process, which uses salt, will ionize the air and clean any dense energy from objects and surfaces, lending the room brightness. It will open this room's energy and allow light in.

After you are done, state aloud, "Spirits of place, please fill this room with high-vibrational light and joy." Quick and easy!

Hop on to amyleighmercree.com/
healinghomebookresources
to get a space-clearing sound
meditation to play in your house!
You can use it in the dining room
and then rest of the house, too.

FENG SHUI IN THE DINING ROOM

The dining room is best balanced with a mixture of yin and yang elements with an emphasis on yin. The touch of yang will keep things lively, and the heavier layer of yin will activate rest and digest in the body and being. To add the yang element, use candles and fire for warmth and ambience. Keep lighting low to create softness and yin. Use fabrics on the tables and perhaps to adorn the windows to bring even more yin to the space. Create an atmosphere of convivial coziness.

Feng Shui Cures in the Dining Room

To enliven the dining room, place some of the cures that follow. Remember that you do not have to do them all at once! Even one or two can have a noticeable effect.

1. The dining room is the heart of the family. It is a place to foster settled chi that is contained. You do this by defining the space. Place a large carpet under the table and make sure the dining room chairs sit on the carpet completely, particularly if the dining area isn't enclosed by walls.

2. We want the chi in the dining room to be slower moving so that everyone can relax, talk, and connect while receiving nutrients. It is smart to emphasize soil chi to accomplish this, since soil is associated with earth. Add symbols of earth and the sun and use earth-toned colors in this area.

3. The metal element has the power to hold chi and contain it in a constructive manner. Round elements, which are also yin, help add this energy. Use some round elements in the decor where it fits. You can also cut a circle out of aluminum foil and hide it under

something. It doesn't have to be visible to add its energy to the dining room.

4. Use wood materials instead of stone to create more yin, especially where you want to spend the most time. Wood is inviting and encourages gathering.

5. Put cushions on the chairs to further slow and relax the chi in this room. This encourages sitting and winding down.

6. Using a round or oval table will contain the chi using the metal element, which will promote communication energetically but also practically, because everyone can see one another.

7. Calm the energy in the room by using lower-height, down-facing lighting. Turn off overhead lights and use lamps with fabric shades, candles, and down-facing, soothing lighting.

8. Create a sanctuary by placing a round bowl of polished rocks in the dining room to bring in a grounded earth element.

9. Place rounded edges everywhere you can, since they create a feeling of safety. Sharp edges feel subconsciously threatening and should be avoided. Shelving and tables are best without pointy edges.

Refer back to The Elements section in the introduction and find out where in the bagua your dining room is located so you can apply those cures to your room, too.

Vastu in the Dining Room

In Vastu, we create a casual, all-accepting dining area. It is meant to be a place to encompass the family and be in warmness and camaraderie.

Vastu Cures

Here are some cures originating in Vastu tradition and writing that you can apply to your dining room:

1. In the Vastu tradition, a rounded table creates an abundance of energy. This will provoke animated conversation. Conversely, a four-sided table will make the environment serene and promote contemplation.
2. In Vastu, the dining room is supposed to be informal. It is believed that excessive formality will not help children learn to share. Therefore, casual settings are best to elevate family togetherness.
3. Layering curtains is encouraged to keep the hot sun out of the space in the heat of the day. It also creates warmth and a homey environment.
4. To symbolize the Vedic zone of tranquility, hang a picture of a respected person or being in your dining room, or use the holy basil plant also known as tulsi, which invokes the spirit of the benevolent deity Vishnu.

Chakra Healing in the Dining Room

We can use the power of chakra healing in the dining room to open up communication and conversation. We can allow the dining room to be a place of joy and lightness. The chakras can help!

Throat Chakra

The throat chakra is located in your neck and is associated with clear communication and expression. An open throat chakra promotes honesty and the ability to feel safe speaking your mind. When families and friends

gather, it's important to make sure that everyone feels confident enough to speak, so an open throat chakra can be a huge help in keeping everyone open and feeling good about sharing their opinions.

Lapis lazuli is a stone that is known for its ability to open the throat chakra. For a long time, lapis lazuli was known for its rarity. It was used to create the lovely royal blue color you see in older paintings. Today, it is said to promote truthful communication. If you are struggling with how to make a point, or how to kindly and tactfully tell your co-worker or partner something you know they won't want to hear, lapis lazuli can help you find just the right words to do so. It brings you spiritual love and hope and resonates strongly with your throat chakra.

Your throat chakra is the control center of your communicative abilities, and red clover blossom is known for unleashing emotions and helping you find words for how you are feeling. Share a cup of red clover blossom tea with a friend or loved one during a difficult conversation and notice how open you feel toward them. You can find red clover blossom all over—just look around for those purple clover flowers you see in backyards or forests. Pick some and place them in a beautiful bud vase in the dining room for a similar effect.

Holistic Health Check

Open the windows frequently to bring fresh air into the space and eliminate VOCs in the atmosphere of your dining room. Remember to check your candles and materials in the room for the toxic elements discussed in the VOC section on page xxxiv. Aim for more natural fibers in the fabrics used as well—that could include fabric tablecloths, napkins, curtains, and upholstery.

CHAPTER 7

LIVING ROOM & DEN

*Y*our living room and den are places of relaxation and leisure. They are very important areas, especially in our exponentially fast-paced world. Everyone in the home needs a place to unwind and let go of the cares of the day.

THE ENERGY OF THE LIVING ROOM

When Dan decided to bring more light energy into the house, he added vanilla essential oil aromatherapy. He also cleared out the clutter in a big way. Piles of magazines from years prior, old DVDs, and unused kids' toys were cleared out of corners. After clearing the clutter, he enlisted the family and they used a DIY clearing ritual to wash the wood floors with a mix of water, white vinegar, lemon essential oil, and clary sage. During this process they opened all of the windows and played some drums to clear the space. Over the next week the whole family gathered in the room more than usual. The room had become drastically more inviting.

AROMATHERAPY FOR THE LIVING ROOM

Using aromatherapy in the living room can help to create a cozy atmosphere. Use warm, sweet scents to inspire a sense of comfort and feelings of security. Use vanilla essential oil to calm and relax the spirit and invoke the feeling of a warm embrace. Adding the scent of cocoa is a good idea too—it can bring richness and sweetness to the room. Enjoy your abundant living room!

LIVING ROOM LEISURE SPRITZ

This easy aromatherapy spray is a great way to create a pleasant atmosphere for family time or the moments you spend relaxing and unwinding. You can diffuse this blend, too.

Ingredients

Spring or distilled water to almost fill the bottle of your choice

10 drops of vanilla essential oil
10 drops of cocoa essential oil
2 drops of cinnamon essential oil

Note: Cinnamon essential oil is not recommended for topical use and is best used sparingly. That said, it smells amazing!

Place all the ingredients into a clean spray bottle and mix well. Remember to shake the bottle well before you use the spray. You can spritz any furniture in the room, such as the couch, curtains, or bookcases. Remember to spritz the corners as well as the center of the living room.

This room is infused with fun and relaxation.
Being in this room allows all family members
to relax and receive rejuvenating energy.
Our family living room is a place of good conversation
and health-enhancing activities.
Everyone has a positive experience and feels a
pleasant sense of belonging in this space.

HOUSEPLANTS FOR THE LIVING ROOM

A pebble plant, also known as Lithops, can add beauty to your living room and its unique appearance can bring imaginativeness and freshness to the room. It looks like a bowl of colorful pebbles! Pebble plant is a succulent that is native to South Africa. Its novel appearance and energy are delightful and make for a fun, decorative accent. This plant thrives in a hot, dry climate so it can be placed in a sunny spot to soak up the heat.

Tiger lilies are fabulous flowers to add to your living room, because they invoke wealth and prosperity. They impart abundance and warmth to the home as well as the energy of health and wellness due to their vibrant color. They infuse the room with their brightness and texture and pump up the energy of having your heart's desires that can really enhance a personal relaxation zone. With tiger lilies ensconced in a vase nearby, it's hard not to feel like you have everything you need—not a bad feeling to have when you're just relaxing in your hard-earned abode.

LIVING ROOM & DEN

CRYSTALS FOR THE LIVING ROOM

Crystals can add a luxurious touch to the living room, which is the seat of your leisure and relaxation time. Not only are they fun decorations that visitors and family alike will enjoy, but they also impart a particular energy that can make you feel even more relaxed than you already would have been after a movie night or just some chill time with your friends.

TIGER'S EYE: This mineral is grounding. It helps your family members find their roots and feel present. It is an enhancement to health and inspires the lower body and organs below the waist, especially, to function optimally. If life has been hectic and you're trying to gather family together to enjoy one another's

company in the living room, consider placing a tiger's eye nearby to help them feel centered.

YELLOW TOURMALINE: This mineral is a harmonizer. It will create a balanced environment in the living room. It is also a cleansing mineral and helps filter out dense energies. That is especially useful if this room is used for looking at screens like televisions, tablets, phones, and computers.

CRYSTALS ARE PEOPLE, TOO

Stones and crystals are alive and deserve care and respect. Guess what? Crystals are living beings! Just like a plant, animal, or person, a crystal has an oversoul and awareness of what's happening to it and its surroundings. It's important that we ask a crystal's permission before we move it or use it for something. To do this, tune in to the crystal by closing your eyes and quieting your mind. Allow yourself to feel answers in the center of your chest as you ask the crystal yes or no questions.

Spirit Helpers

How can you call upon spirit energy to bring your family together and help everyone relax together in the living room? You'll want an entity that promotes stability, so the goddess Freya's energy is helpful to tap into. Freya is a Norse goddess who is partnered with the deity Odin. These two beings are available to bring harmony to the home. They also impart prosperity and relationship success, so Odin and Freya are a great couple to turn toward if you and your partner use the living room to recharge.

Meditation to Invoke the Energies of Freya and Odin

Freya helps us create and appreciate beauty and abundance. She resonates with the magnetism and receptive qualities of the divine feminine. She teaches us to communicate clearly and with ease. She brings empowerment to women and supports childbirth and fertility.

Odin is a pillar of strength as well as caring and kindness. He holds the essence of masculine presence and attention. He brings steadiness and grounded energy to the living room. These two beings have many gifts to offer all members of the family.

As a unit, Freya and Odin are a matched pair and embody the harmony of the sacred feminine and masculine in partnership. They bring balance and can ignite sensual fireworks as appropriate. They are also fruitful and plentiful and attract the energy of wealth.

Say the following affirmation aloud: "I invite the power and presence of Freya and Odin to infuse the matter and energy of this space. This room is filled with harmony and beauty and attracts prosperity to the house and household. All that occurs here and in this home is watched over by Freya and Odin and for the highest good of all life, helping all and harming none. I invite Freya and Odin to guide the lives of the inhabitants of this home and create ease, harmony, wealth, and joy here and in our lives. It is done." "The living room is the social center of your abode. It's a great idea to summon spirits to help you enjoy it."

Spirits of Place

Connect with the spirits who are responsible for the land over which your living room is built. Ask these beings to bring harmony and prosperity to your life and being. State aloud in the living room, "I ask that all that transpires in this room be for the highest good of all life and in accordance with universal natural law, helping all, harming none. Please infuse this living room with love and comfort. Help all who enter to relax and recharge here and live in joy and harmony."

Animal Helpers

The living room is the perfect place for the animal spirit of the lion. Lions are pack animals, and you can allow the energy of the lion pride to infuse your space. Imagine lions companionably cuddling in the savanna and then, as needed, springing into action and easily hunting delicious prey. In an ideal situation, they have leisure time and are prosperous and plentiful. You can say aloud, "I welcome the energy of the lion pride to elevate this space to one of ease, rest, companionship, and abundance. Thank you for your presence, dear lion friends."

ROOTS IN THE EARTH
LIVING ROOM RITUAL

Use the following ritual to help you get in touch with the roots that connect you to the planet, that nourish and sustain you. A version of this was originally shared with me by my late medicine teacher, Laurie. Read this aloud or quietly to yourself in the living room. If your family members are interested, they can participate. This ritual is great for kids of all ages.

Place your attention on the soles of your feet. Imagine roots growing out of each foot and out of your tailbone; send them into the earth. They may combine into one large root or remain as two or three separate roots. All of these variations are fine, and you do not have to know which one is happening as you do the ritual. Feel these roots growing deeper and deeper through soil and dirt, through a matrix of rock and stone and through aquifers full of water. Continue growing your roots down through the magma into the mantle of the planet. Finally, grow them into the core of the earth. Feel them sucked into the inner core of the planet. Feel how held, stable, strong, and rooted you are. Attune to the energy and vibration of the earth flowing up through your roots and into your feet and tailbone. Feel it pulsing within you. Hear the inner heartbeat of the planet. Hear it beating like a gentle drum. Merge with this interdimensional sound. Experience deep communion with the earth. Feel her love for you expand into each cell in your body. All is right with you and your mother, the earth. She has infinite strength and she shares this wellspring of stability and strength with you, her child. Thank the earth for this huge gift. Experience what it feels like to be fully present and grounded in the moment, in the *now*. Say aloud, "Let presence and grounding pervade this room and create family and personal harmony and enhance the health of all who enter."

FENG SHUI IN THE LIVING ROOM

The living room is most enhanced with a mixture of yin and yang elements with an emphasis on yin. A tiny bit of yang will keep things lively but major emphasis on yin will activate relaxation and feelings of security. To add a dash of yang element, use candles and a fireplace for heat and light. Choose soft lighting to make the yin elements more prominent. Dimmer switches are excellent for this purpose. Focus on soft fabrics and textures and think kinesthetically. What fabrics feel cozy and enveloping? Use plenty of pillows and cushy surfaces to invite lounging and lying down. Choose plush rugs to define the space.

If a room is big and echolike, it can be too yang, as are elements like tiles, hard surfaces, and starkness. Use a large, sumptuous carpet to define the room as if the carpet is a smaller room within the room. So place the furniture on the rug to create a bubble of yin. Yin reduces family arguments and conflict and allows for ease of communication.

Feng Shui Cures in the Living Room

To make your living room a cozy place to be, try some of the cures below.

1. All of the wonderful, inviting yin elements in the room, like couches and pillows, accumulate chi. Be sure to keep them clean and energetically clear by vacuuming and periodically airing them out on a sunlit patio if possible.

2. The living room is a key place in the home where the family chi merges together to create a whole. If the chi moves too quickly, it can be disruptive, and people in the home may find it hard to settle down. We want an even, constant flow of chi that is more horizontal than vertical. This encourages harmony. If the chi is a bit more toward the downward direction, then the family will be able to feel settled in together more easily. This can be accomplished by eschewing upward lighting and choosing to create a grounded atmosphere.

3. If you want to help the family settle disputes more easily and get things done, add eastern chi, which is emphasized by green and wood items. To add sensitivity to the space, use dark green and align the room's layout with the southeast. To amp up southern fiery expressiveness, use reds, pinks, and warm-toned purples. To create caring and healthy interdependence in the home, use southwest energy and earth elements like stone and soil, as well as earth-toned colors. Western chi invokes playfulness and connection through laughter. If you'd like to add this energy, decorate your space with pictures of lakes, pink items, and metal materials. Dignity, respect, and intentional action is associated with the northwest in Taoism, so if this is what you want your living room to emphasize, use silver, gray, and warm white to decorate. North chi is independent and free, so if you'd like to add

more of that energy, use water and shiny elements. And to empower you and the other people in the house to be clear and direct, use northeast chi by adding shiny white to your decor.

4. To activate health energy for all, use yellow, earth tones, and things from the earth. Choose square-shaped objects or design layouts and more horizontal elements.

5. If a conflict is impending, take it outside! In feng shui, it is suggested that if you wish to avoid contaminating the energy of the home, avoid conflict inside of it whenever possible. And if you are having a difficult discussion, consider sitting side by side instead of across from one another. This creates a more teamlike, less oppositional atmosphere.

6. If an argument happens in the home, clean up the chi in and around the house. Open the windows afterward to clear the energy and add some sea salt to

the floor or carpet to soak up the chi and then vacuum or sweep it up before emptying it outdoors.

7. To reduce family arguments, decrease the number of mirrors in the home. They bounce chi around and foster conflict. Plus, add more yin and reduce sharp corners. Choose rounded edges whenever possible.

8. Make sure all of the personalities in the home are represented and validated. Let kids pick out some small elements and decor even if you have a more set decorating scheme in place.

9. Fountains are a feng shui favorite. The presence of water brings prosperity to the home, and the movement in a fountain adds chi flow. In addition, sound is a chi enhancer. Fountains represent a steady flow of chi and money and are a source of prosperity and abundance. They work in this way without even being plugged in all of the time. Keep the fountain full

to the brim and clean it often, and it will be a money magnet. If possible, place it in the wealth area of the bagua or the back left corner of the room relative to the entrance to the room.

> Refer back to The Elements section in the introduction and find out where in the bagua your living room is located and apply those cures to your room, too.

VASTU IN THE LIVING ROOM

The living room can be a sanctuary for the whole family that fosters togetherness. This is the essence of Vastu, creating meaning and sanctuary. The living room can also be a place of quiet solitude and leisure as well as entertainment and fun.

Vastu Living Room Cures

Use these suggestions to bring the healing power of Vastu to your living room or den:

1. To minimize time spent in front of the television, place it in the northwest corner of the room, which is symbolic of the element air and quick movement. This will inspire a restless feeling when you are looking at the TV and make you want to move on to something else.

2. Alternately, you can place the television on the southeast side of the room, which symbolizes fire. Northwest or southeast placement will help prevent the TV from being an energetic drain on the home and on family time and well-being.

3. In Vastu, it is recommended that you try to foster a welcoming and friendly feeling in the living room, which will make it ideal for relaxation. To achieve this, it is recommended that a bit of everyone who resides there is represented, so everyone's vibrational frequency is present there—again, don't shut your kids or your partner out of the design process, even if you have a decorating scheme. Let them pick out a few small items so that everyone has a say in how the living room is decorated.

4. Bringing life to the space is also a Vastu principle. To keep the living room feeling alive, try adding stone sculptures, clay pots, and living plants.

LET THERE BE LIGHT!

Open all of the shades and curtains each morning to expose the family to natural light, which can help balance production of the sleep hormone melatonin. The sunlight will also cleanse your home's chi.

CHAKRA HEALING IN THE HOME

Chakra healing in the living room can be helpful in regulating the nervous system and allowing you to relax more deeply. Opening to serenity makes space for you and anyone with whom you live to go more deeply within.

Crown Chakra

It's normal to hope that time spent in the living room will lead you to balance, relaxation, and perhaps just a bit of enlightenment. The crown chakra is located at the top of your head and is associated with insight and cosmic energy. A balanced crown chakra will lead to feelings of spiritual connection and well-being—not a bad thing to reach for when you hunker down for some me time on the couch.

Amethyst is a stone well known for its deep purple color and its lovely sparkle. You'll often find it in jewelry, but it is more than just a decorative gem. Amethyst promotes inner peace and balances your psychic and physical energies. It brings inner strength and opens you up to spiritual insight. Amethyst is also known for its powers in helping with sobriety, so use it when you are trying to rid yourself of addictive behaviors. Can't go to bed without a glass or two of wine and want to shake that habit? Put an amethyst on your bookshelf and commit to relaxing through other means.

There are other ways to balance your crown chakra through contemplation or relaxation. For thousands of years, countless cultures have used frankincense to aid in meditation, purification, and other activities related to the crown chakra. Frankincense targets areas of your brain that help you feel more open and able to connect with great ideas. It is a great spiritual cleanser and will make you more receptive to metaphysical forces and the positive influence of the greater universe. You can display its resin in the home and light it as you choose to further emanate its goodness.

HOLISTIC HEALTH CHECK

Take some time to research the fabrics in your upholstered furniture. You don't have to replace them all at once, but think about which pillows, blankets, and furniture might be ready to be replaced next and be prepared to choose healthy, organic fabrics and materials to slowly overhaul the health of the space.

PART 4

PRODUCTIVITY & CREATIVITY

*I*n this section, we'll delve deeply into the areas of the home where you work and create. We will set up each room for abundance. Whether you want to accumulate wealth and prosperity in your life or just boost your performance at work, there are plenty of ways to push the energy of your home in the direction of success. When you work in the areas that we make over, you'll be working toward a future in which your reputation for skill at your craft is assured.

Additionally, we will explore your artistic and creative sides. In this section we will investigate both the creative process and its execution. You'll love the results you can get when you try some of these cures and follow this advice and you'll see the results—whether through dancing, singing, solving problems creatively, or finding ways of thinking outside of the box to better your life.

CHAPTER 8

HOME OFFICE

Many of us are working in our home offices most or all of our working hours. It is more crucial than ever that we upgrade the space. This area can bring us prosperity and efficiency. There are so many wonderful ways to amp up our wealth and improve our reputation and level of fame.

THE ENERGY OF THE HOME OFFICE

The home office can bring money to your home not only through your efforts but also though your energy. One client of mine posted a list of wealth-building and career-affirming statements in the home office. For twenty-one days she said them aloud daily upon entering and leaving. She noticed a marked uptick in her freelance business and liked the practice so much that she continued it indefinitely. When affirming your wealth and joy becomes a habit, amazing thigs happen.

AROMATHERAPY FOR THE HOME OFFICE

Scent can increase focus and productivity. Even though you might not initially notice fragrance in the air, just a subtle hint of certain smells can improve mental clarity and prompt the inspiration you need to solve problems in a creative way. Rosemary essential oil is good for all of those things and it has numerous health benefits, too. It boosts circulation and even stimulates hair growth. It brings mental alertness and imparts a lively sense of cognitive focus.

Black pepper essential oil is another enlivening and wonderful oil that awakens the senses. It's also an anti-viral and antimicrobial powerhouse, which is great if you don't want to get sidelined by illness while you're trying to hit a deadline or put together an important presentation.

AWESOME OFFICE SUCCESS AND PROSPERITY SPRITZ

Use this easy aromatherapy spray to create an invigorating office environment and attract wealth into your life and home. Spritz it on your office chair and furniture and as an air freshener. You can also diffuse this blend. You can use it topically as an abundance-attracting body spray as well.

Ingredients

Spring or distilled water to almost fill the bottle of your choice

10 drops of sandalwood essential oil
5 drops of frankincense essential oil
5 drops of myrrh essential oil
10 drops of ginger essential oil

Place all the ingredients into a clean spray bottle and mix well.
Shake the bottle before each use.

Healing Power Mantras

I am known for my success and skill.

Wealth comes to me easily and effortlessly.

Money loves me! Money is my supportive friend, and I am grateful.

I am abundant, rich, prosperous, and filled with joy.

HOUSEPLANTS FOR THE HOME OFFICE

Envision a forest of tall, thick bamboo with the breeze blowing through it, creating a light, soothing, percussive sound. A potted bamboo plant is a wonderful way to bring that peace into your home office. It is a feng shui staple for a reason! Its hollow stalks create more movement of chi in the home. Eight stalks attract prosperity and nine magnetize fortune and great luck.

If you're looking to add a vase of flowers to your office to keep your search for success active, narcissus flowers add the energy of wealth and luxury. They bring prosperity and opulence to the home. They are associated with the water element in Taoism and invoke the water element, which includes properties of money and success. Narcissus blooms also have an intoxicating and exotic scent that magnetizes career achievements and enhances your professional reputation. Think rock star career energy!

CRYSTALS FOR THE HOME OFFICE

You can use crystals to decorate your home office and add some oomph to its energy. You can place them on windowsills and on your desk. You can display them in decorative glass and ceramic dishes.

GREEN QUARTZ: This mineral fosters creativity, plus it attracts success, abundance, prosperity, and wealth! It's a pretty good all-around crystal for the home office, whether you use that space as a full work-from-home setup or just to check your stocks or balance your budget.

GREEN TOURMALINE: This mineral inspires compassion, which is a beautiful  and abundant enhancement to life. At the same time, it is a wealth and prosperity powerhouse and creates heart-based success and abundance. It helps us become wealthy and creates a better world in the process, so it's a great way to assure yourself of a great life that is still ethical and kind to other people and the earth.

Spirit Helpers

To do well in your job, you need to work hard, but undeniably, you also need luck. There are many good luck spirits, gods, and other entities, but foremost among them is the Hindu deity Lakshmi. Lakshmi is a goddess primarily known as the bringer of good fortune. She can help you attract success, wealth, and receive your heart's desires. She helps you relax into the benevolence of life and allows serendipity to enter your dealings. She brings you money and ease so you can live a rich and full life. She also makes you effective and efficient at your job so you can acquire the recognition and reward you desire while letting it be easy and effortless.

Meditation to Invoke the Energy of Lakshmi

Say the following affirmation aloud: "I invoke Lakshmi to bring me maximum success and wealth coupled with fun, adventure, leisure, and balance. All that occurs in this office is blessed by Lakshmi and creates prosperity and positive fame for me and for the highest good of all life, helping all and harming none. I invite Lakshmi to guide the lives of the inhabitants of this home and create wealth, success, ease, and joy here and in our lives. It is done."

Spirits of Place

Allow yourself to connect with the spirits who are responsible for the land over which your home office is built. Ask these beings to bring success and prosperity to your life and being. State aloud in the office, "I ask that all that transpires in this room be for the highest good of all life and in accordance with universal natural law, helping all, harming none. Please infuse this office with financial rewards and success. Help all who enter to feel inspired and capable here and receive wealth and triumph."

Animal Helpers

The home office is enhanced by the animal spirit of the horse. Horses bring empowerment and confidence. Think of them wild and running free. They are muscular and full of strength. Imagine horses and their energy of triumph and light. They are synonymous with success and positive fame. You can say aloud, "I invoke the energy of powerful horses full of confidence and easy success to elevate this space to one of prosperity, flow, victory, and abundance. Thank you for your presence, dear horse friends."

Connecting Water and Metal Ritual

I created this ritual for my own use, and it has brought me lots of success, so I wanted to share it with you. In Taoism, as you read earlier, there are five elements. The Taoist cycle begins with the element of wood, then fire, earth, metal, and water. The metal area is especially present in the house in the zone of the bagua for attracting helpers. That is the front right corner of the home.

The water element is present in several areas of the bagua and it is very strong in the prosperity section. It is a super important area. This area is the back, left area of the bagua. Identify these two areas and then think about attracting helpers to the area of wealth. What wonderful things might happen if you activate that energy?

Energy follows intention. This ritual requires no material except your own body and mind. You will connect these two sections of the home with your physical presence and amplify the resulting energy with your mind.

Start in the helpful people area. Clap your hands six times, because that is the number for that area of the bagua. Say aloud, "I activate and accept help and benevolence from life, people, and the universe. Thank you!" Next, walk in the straightest line you can back to the prosperity corner. When you get to the wealth area, clap eight times and say, "My wealth and prosperity are growing and multiplying, and I am grateful."

Now, begin pacing deliberately back and forth between these two areas. Say the following mantra aloud as you walk: "I strengthen and activate the helpers in my life and the energy of abundance and money with each step." Feel the line you are walking reverberating with each pass. Increase your speed and activate that area like you are plucking a string on a musical instrument. Feel the energy resonating, amplifying, and building. Keep going until you feel the energy resonating with strength and power. If you want to amp it up even more, do this nine or ninety-nine times, because nine is a power number in feng shui. When this ritual is complete, go to the midpoint of the line you walked at the center of the house and stand. Sense the energy you've accumulated and say "Thank you" aloud nine times.

Feng Shui in the Home Office

The office is best enhanced with a mixture of yin and yang elements, with an emphasis on yang. A tiny bit of yin will holistically contain the energy so it doesn't leak out of the room, but a major emphasis on yang will create action and movement. For yin, you can use an area rug that holds the desk and chair and/or a cushy seat on your chair if you sit at your desk. To foster the yang, you will want to create a space with clean and shiny surfaces, like hardwood floors, a sturdy desk, firm surfaces, and natural materials.

Feng Shui Office Cures

Here is a selection of cures for your home office. As always, you do not have to do them all at once—try applying one or two and then working in the office for a few days to see whether you can determine a difference. If you like what you feel, add more.

1. Use the bagua to your advantage! Envision placing it over the room and add some important elements in key areas. Put representations of water or a fountain in the back, left-hand corner of the room to keep wealth and abundance energy flowing. And remember to keep that fountain topped up! Pro tip: use distilled water to keep the fountain clean and free of minerals and sediment.

2. The left side of the room, about halfway to the back, is the family area. In addition to being key for family relationships, it also governs household expenses and is a money-generating spot. Use the wood element here, and the color green. If you are good at caring for plants, place a tall, columnar-shaped plant here, like bamboo.

3. The entrance to the room is where the chi enters and is equivalent to the front door of the house. It is also a water element place, and its best color is black. Put a water image in place by the entrance. It's even better if the water looks like it is flowing in from the direction of the door. For example, a waterfall picture is great—it brings a cascade of blessing and fortune into the room.

4. Put your educational materials and books on the front right wall to enhance your knowledge in that area of the bagua.

5. Straight ahead to the back wall is where the energy of your reputation lives. Juice it up with lights, candles, the color red, heat, and tall triangular items. Also, you can display your certificates and accolades there.

6. You can foster good working relationships in the back, righthand corner of the room. Place items in twos and use a bit of pink. Consider writing an affirmative statement on paper and hide it. Try something like, "I get along with my colleagues and I am well liked and respected. My co-workers promote me and recognize me."

7. Place your desk in the position of power. Make sure it faces the entrance and has a strong wall behind it (but not too close to it) and, ideally, an open vista in front of it.

8. You can also place the bagua over your desk. Optimize the surface of your desk by decorating with colors and symbols representing energy you want to amplify in their corresponding areas.

9. Consider a standing desk to promote health and eliminate neck and back pain. Standing is better for you in numerous ways: circulation, metabolic burn, spinal align-

ment, and more. I like to place my laptop at shoulder height so I can look straight ahead, not down, and avoid "texting neck."

Refer back to The Elements section in the introduction and find out where in the bagua your home office is located and apply those cures to your room, too.

VASTU IN THE HOME OFFICE

Vastu places a major emphasis on bringing spiritualty into the home. It is also a big proponent of not overworking. It is all about balance and meaning. So this perspective can be equanimous in a world of overworking.

1. In Vastu, it is thought to be ideal to have the home office or study placed in the east, north, or west of the home. If it is in the south, then use the Vastu practice of making an offering to the deities that can help balance energy. Place a symbol of the Hindu goddess of wealth, Lakshmi, in the south. You can also select a being from another faith tradition or culture that represents success. For example, you could make an offering to the goddess Nike, who is a symbol of victory. Make sure the offering is specific to the deity—so gold coins for Lakshmi and items or pictures with wings for Nike.

2. To improve focus, keep televisions and other distractions out of this space. Vastu is wise in emphasizing limiting television and technology from the home in general. These items distract us from healthy, social, relaxing, and productive activities and can be addictive and inspire us to use our time in valueless ways.

3. Vastu empathizes balance and a well-rounded lifestyle with an emphasis on the spiritual. As such, it is recommended that you create a soulful and peaceful atmosphere even in the office to remind you of the truth of your being. This can be especially useful when trying to maintain work-life balance!

HOME OFFICE

Symbols of Success
for the Office

Fill your office with symbols of success! Tap into the power of mythology and consider adding representations of those who evoke your imagination and inspire you. Consider adding images or sculptures of these deities and gods who represent good fortune, success, wealth, and prosperity:

» Libertas, Roman goddess of freedom

» Artemis, Greek goddess of independence

» Aje, Yoruba goddess of wealth

» Oshun, another Yoruba goddess of financial fortune as well as love

» Fortuna, Roman goddess of good luck and fortunes

» Anumati, Hindu goddess of wealth

» Daikokr, Shinto god of luck and money

» Esme, Welsh goddess of wealth and protection

» Po Tai, the laughing Buddha who is a Buddhist deity of money and prosperity

HOME OFFICE

CHAKRA HEALING IN THE HOME OFFICE

Your chakras can be a huge help in your career success. You can become more present and grounded in your body and create what you desire in the physical world.

Earth Star Chakra

The earth star chakra is located several feet below your feet and is associated with earthly energies and stability. It connects you to your soul's past incarnations and creates a sense of being one with the earth. It is essential to be connected to the earth in a deep manner to receive and align with material success and resources.

Dravite is a form of brown tourmaline that possesses protective energies. It combats anxiety and stresses, helping you feel stable and relaxed in difficult situations. Dravite is known for its role as a protector of the home, which makes it the ideal earth star chakra stone, connecting you to your home on earth and keeping you grounded and centered. Use it when you feel unstable or to initiate a new home or office after a major move.

When in the ground, wintergreen absorbs and retains energies from the earth that can help you feel centered and balanced, so it's a great herb to use to balance your earth star chakra. Use it when you need to remind yourself about the beauty of nature and the world, or when the busy pace of modern life is getting too overwhelming for you. It brings spectacular balance to the home office. You can place it in a bowl or vase and display its leaves, berries, and flowers. They all smell divine!

HOLISTIC HEALTH CHECK

Take a look around your office and remove any VOC-generating items. For example, check to see if you have any paraffin candles or plastic items. What plastics could you replace with healthier options? And what synthetic fabrics might be able to be switched out for natural fibers when you are ready to replace them? Make it part of your daily routine to open the windows when you start your day and close them and your office door at the end of the day, for the added psychological benefit of preventing your work worries from following you after you finish.

CHAPTER 9

LIBRARY & STUDY

Even if you do not have a library or study, you may have an area where you read, store books, or devote to learning. A lot of these suggestions will apply and many would work well in a child's homework area, too. A music room would also benefit from many of the suggestions that follow.

THE ENERGY OF THE LIBRARY

Devotion to learning and intellectual curiosity are wonderful additions to the home. Reigniting the love of the written word is incredibly crucial. Children whose parents read to them even before they understand learn to associate reading with feelings of warmth and happiness. If you or family members are readers, this place will become a treasured spot. Even if you are not, it is great for all to have an area to enjoy and learn without any pressure or obligation, but for the sheer joy of learning or creating.

AROMATHERAPY

You can use aromatic essential oils in the library, study, or area where you like to read, challenge your brain, practice a musical instrument, or improve your knowledge base. Eucalyptus oil is enlivening and improves cognition. It is also antiviral, antimicrobial, and antibacterial. Eucalyptus oil is best used aromatherapeutically but not applied topically because it can irritate skin.

BOOK READING BLISS SPRITZ

This easy aromatherapy spray helps you to think more clearly,
mprove your memory, and learn more efficiently.
Spritz it on furniture and as an air freshener.
You can also diffuse this blend.
Because you will make this with organic,
therapeutic-grade essential oils, it will be 100 percent healthy!
You can use it topically as a body spray that promotes the good fortune
brought by spearmint and
calmness for the nervous system imparted by lavender.

Ingredients

Spring or distilled water to almost fill the bottle of your choice

20 drops of spearmint essential oil
5 drops of lavender essential oil

Place all the ingredients into a clean spray bottle and mix well.
Shake well before each use.

HOUSEPLANTS FOR THE LIBRARY

A bonsai plant promotes ease and grace. Bonsai is a technique that can be used to shape a variety of plant species into beautiful forms. The process can be time-consuming and requires attention to detail, care, and knowledge. This plant symbolizes achievement because its cultivation is such a painstaking process; its presence indicates discipline. Because this plant requires regular care, it is the perfect addition to a study or library—and an excellent way to add contemplation and restraint to the most studious area of your home.

An iris is another great form of plant life to add to your library. The iris symbolizes intelligence because it is named after the Greek goddess of the rainbow, who is the bringer of wisdom from the gods. Iris flowers can be displayed to boost the chi of the room and open the mind to knowledge and new ideas.

CRYSTALS FOR THE LIBRARY

Crystals are fascinating objects to study, and their energy can give back to any space in your home that requires mental concentration. Try these:

JASPER: This mineral balances the mind and brings a nurturing energy into the home. It is a protective and cleansing stone and is wonderful to have in the library area. Cleanse this stone in the sun.

MOLDAVITE: This stone is extraterrestrial in origin. It was created in an area of Czechoslovakia via a meteoric event. This mineral helps you see clearly and can assist you in connecting with expanded ideas of reality—it is an excellent stone for opening yourself up to visionary, new ideas!

SPIRIT HELPERS

In the area of your home where you and your family gather knowledge and hone your skills, it is helpful to call upon the energy of a being that represents an expansive worldview, which will give you the motivation to overcome your obstacles and seek new challenges. Libertas is the Roman goddess of liberty. She is a governess of freedom, both inner and outer. In fact, the word *libertas* is the Latin word for "freedom." When depicted in paintings or sculptures, Libertas is sometimes pictured wearing a crown of laurel leaves or a liberty cap or crown and carrying a pole of liberty called a *vindicta*. The well-known philosopher Cicero wrote about a temple that was built in her honor on Aventine Hill in Rome.

Meditation to Invoke the Energy of Libertas

It is time for you to feel the true inner feeling of freedom. Does your heart feel free? Do you feel liberated to do what you need and choose? Ask yourself these questions knowing that you are worthy of freedom, for you will choose benevolent actions and situations. Trust yourself to be kind and compassionate while also fulfilling your personal liberty. You already have or can acquire the knowledge you need to create the life you desire. Libertas will help you gather it.

infuse this area with wisdom and an appreciation of art and knowledge. Help all who enter to feel inspired and capable here and integrate knowledge into the attainment of my heart's desires."

Say the following affirmation aloud: "Dear Libertas, please help me see and feel my inner freedom and boundlessness. Empower me to gather the knowledge and skills I need to live my joyful sovereignty. It is done."

Spirits of Place

Allow yourself to connect with the spirits who are responsible for the land over which your library or learning area is built. Ask these beings to bring knowledge and inspiration to your life and soul. State aloud in the study or library, "I ask that all that transpires in this room be for the highest good of all life and in accordance with universal natural law, helping all, harming none. Please

Animal Helpers

The spirit of the elephant can enhance your library and study if you invoke its presence. Elephants impart wisdom and empathy. They are incredibly intelligent animals known for being compassionate and are said to be able to understand the passage of time. They project strength and kindness, and they are protective of their own and will keep the inhabitants of your home feeling safe and supported. Imagine elephants in a dignified processional of wise beings walking with purpose. Picture elephant parents cuddling their young ones. You can say aloud, "I invoke the energy of wise elephants full of supportive energy and empathy. Thank you for your presence, dear elephant friends."

Sweet Clover
Smoke Ritual

Sweet clover imparts a lightness that can be very much appreciated in the library, where intense mental concentration can become overwhelming. We can add this breezy energy to the library or study and alchemize it by safely burning it. Gather sweet clover in your yard if you live in a region where it grows, although make sure you are certain of the plant! You may also be able to obtain clover at an herbal shop. You will want to dry the stalks with the leaves and any flowers still attached (if you are working with fresh clover that hasn't already been dried). To do this, place the stalks lengthwise in a bundle. You can tie them together at the bottom with a piece of cotton string. Hang the bundle upside down for a few days until it is mostly dry.

Once your dried clover is ready, get a fire-safe bowl or a large shell made for smoke cleansing and carefully light a small amount of the bundle. Start the fire over the sink and proceed very carefully, monitoring the flames. Blow out the fire a few moments after it starts and let it smolder. Then take it into the study or library area.

Waft the smoke through the area and make sure the windows are open and the area is well ventilated. State out loud, "This area is full of inspirations, relaxation, and the pleasure of learning."

FENG SHUI IN THE LIBRARY

The library area can be wonderfully enhanced with a mixture of yin and yang elements, with an emphasis on yin. Plenty of yin will promote a cozy atmosphere for reading, learning, and creating. A tiny bit of yang will keep your mind active and ready to synthesize information. For yin, add a plush area rug, ideally made out of natural materials. A sumptuous reading chair, couch, or chaise is also a good addition. To cultivate yang energy, you can use wooden tables or shelves to bring  solidness and sturdiness. Wood is perfect because it is not too aggressively yang and has a bit of an underlying yin element.

Feng Shui Library Cures

To optimize the library or study, these cures should do the trick. They'll leave you, your family, and your guests feeling as if the house has a cerebral center

where deep contemplation is easy to accomplish.

1. Add natural elements to your home. They add chi and beauty! Try shells, rocks, driftwood, even coral. Happy travel memories might also be attached to some of these items depending on where you collected them.

2. Add warmth to your study with pure beeswax candles. They generate negative ions and make you feel healthy and liberated.

3. Add images of lushness. Rich nature energy can be added through pictures and art. Earthy landscapes will bring abundance and grounding to the room and house.

4. If you are blending two or more families in the home, take a group picture and place it in a wooden frame to help the family create roots together and thrive as a new family unit.

5. Place a circular bowl of smooth stones you collected in the area.

The bowl is round for yin energy. The smooth stones bring the grounding energy  of the earth indoors. This item will help calm down the space and help anyone in it slow down to relax, learn, and read.

6. The "sharp" edges of bookshelves are disruptive to the good energy of the area. To soften the edges, you can cover them with glass or wooden doors, or even more easily, pull all of the books to the front edge of the shelves.

7. Clear your literary clutter by sharing or donating books that you will not read or reference again. Make space on your bookshelves to allow new knowledge and talents to be activated. Be intentional with all of your cures. In this case, ask yourself from an energetic and life perspective: what do you want to add to that newly open area?

8. To revitalize and add mental clarity to the home's energy, temporarily tie some sprigs of fresh rosemary to a broom and use it to sweep the area clean. Don't forget the corners! Clear out old dusty energy with the broom while the rosemary fills the area with powerful intellectual energy.

9. If you can't settle down in the area, check for environmental elements with anxious energy like: harsh overhead lighting, fluorescent or LED lighting, bright white walls, and overly yang surroundings. To settle the energy, consider a heavier piece of furniture. Use soft fabrics and upholstery to add yin and/or add wood to soften and foster growing and evolution. Wood means new growth, but in a softer, less frenetic way than more aggressive materials like metal or glass.

Refer back to The Elements section in the introduction and find out where in the bagua your library area is located and apply those cures to your room, too.

Vastu in the Library

Vastu is greatly in favor of the promotion of knowledge. It is a way that balance can be brought to the home and serenity fostered.

1. In Vastu, it is thought to be ideal to refrain from placing televisions or too many devices in the study or library. An exception would be if a device is part of learning or creative expression. In that case, it is good to turn it off and even remove or cover it when it is not in use.

2. Vastu promotes balance. It is believed that a well-rounded life is crucial, and work should be in proportion with learning, family, creative pleasure, romance, rest, and all of your other priorities. Create a library or study that is relaxing and calming and generally fits in with the rest of your life.

3. The study is meant to be a spiritual refuge for the soul in the realm of learning. In Vastu, each room is meant to hold a dash or more of spir-

ituality. Vastu is a soulful philosophy for living. Consider how you could add a bit of heart and soul to the space. What would add that touch of meaning for you? A figurine of a favorite animal? Or a piece of art that moves you? Consider, and then add some soul in whatever way makes sense to you.

Chakra Healing in the Library

We can enhance the energy of the chakras to promote knowledge and understanding. Infusing the chakras with bright, white light and healing can allow us to open to higher levels of consciousness.

Soul Star Chakra

The soul star chakra is located several feet above your head and is associated with spiritual growth and enlighten-ment. It connects you to the larger metaphysical universe and leaves you

open to communication from higher powers and forces.

To open the soul star chakra, it's important to clear your head of distractions and promote understanding. Selenite is a wonderful crystal for getting to the point and reaching for new insights. Also known as Desert Rose, selenite is a transparent stone that comes from the Greek word for "moon." It is a stone of mental clarity, enhancing your mental flexibility and accessing the energy of your subconscious mind. Many people use selenite to contact and communicate with angels or spirit guides. It removes energy blocks, so it is a great stone to use to heighten the effects of other stones. It is also a very soft stone, so it can be molded or carved very easily to suit your purposes.

To balance the soul star chakra, consider a healing herb like angelica. Angelica, as its name would suggest, has long been associated with angels. It can be used to protect against negative influences and is known for opening you up to greater spiritual awareness. Though angelica is a fabulous herb, it is not ideal for all situations. If you are pregnant, be careful to avoid angelica, as it can have long-term effects on gestation and the health of your pregnancy and your child.

Holistic Health Check

You might like to make the library a place that is full of—radical concept—printed books! They relax you more than screens with blue light. Consider how to create a space full of natural elements and relaxing items. Do a sweep to remove any items with fragrances that are not exclusively derived from essential oils. If your library doesn't have windows, consider adding an air purifier to keep the air quality high and any allergens low.

CHAPTER 10

MEDITATION ROOM

A meditation area brings a space of divine calm to the home. This zone is an opening to spirit and an inspiration for mindfulness. Even if you do not have a dedicated room, you may have an area where you meditate and indulge in spiritual practices and contemplation. A lot of these suggestions will apply wonderfully.

THE ENERGY OF THE MEDITATION ROOM

Your meditation area might be a space where you create an altar or focus zone where you can connect with something bigger than yourself. It is an area to align with nonphysical beings. Many people love the addition of an altar space and find they experience more feelings of spiritual transcendence when they have a spot to focus and dedicate to their spiritual life. Some people use divination cards in these areas or add fresh flowers and symbols of the expanded universe that resonate with them in particular. An altar is an individual thing. Make yours your own.

Aromatherapy for the Meditation Room

You can use essential oils in your meditation area and create a tranquil and refined space. Carrot seed essential oil is a great scent for tapping into your intuition because it increases clairvoyance.

Fir oil brings inspiration and heightens spiritual awareness. It also activates the kidney meridian, preventing stagnation and keeping the chi moving. This helps prevent ailments related to stagnant kidney chi, like urinary tract infections and more.

MINDFUL MEDITATION SERENE SPRITZ

This light and fresh aromatherapy spray helps you to sink into meditation and access your intuition. Spritz it on furniture, cushions, and linens and use it as an air freshener. You can also diffuse this blend or use it topically as a body spray that promotes transcendent states and stillness.

Ingredients

Spring or distilled water to almost fill the bottle of your choice

10 drops of helichrysum essential oil
10 drops of mandarin essential oil

Place all the ingredients into a clean spray bottle and mix well.
Shake well before each use.

Houseplants for the Meditation Room

A morning glory flowering houseplant is a lovely addition to a meditation space.

This plant's energy brings intuition into the forefront of your consciousness and opens you to the delicate and insightful side of life.

Healing Power Mantras

I easily sink deeply into the inner quiet of my being for my highest good.
Spiritual knowledge, expansion, and evolution infuse me and this space.
I choose to evolve spiritually and as a compassionate, loving human being
and allow this space and my home to support this process.
I feel and experience the great beyond and receive new
cosmic knowledge with gratitude.

Magnolia flowers are another great addition to your spiritual space. Magnolias bring wisdom and help increase the spiritual in a room. They aid in meditation and contemplative spirituality and help you see the love and divinity in all beings. If you happen to have a magnolia tree outside your house or building, you can trim the flowers from the trees with care. In that case, ask the plant's permission first. Do this by quieting your mind and standing near the plant in question. Close your eyes and attune to the plant. Ask your question gently and be open to the answer flowing forth from the plant to you. You can gently touch the plant as needed to increase the connection. Plants are living beings who deserve our utmost care and respect.

CRYSTALS FOR THE MEDITATION ROOM

Use the following mineral to enhance the energy of your meditation:

ELECTRIC BLUE SHEEN OBSIDIAN: This mineral is a black obsidian with a sheen of electric blue. It fosters healing and assists in shamanic journeying. It stimulates visionary experiences and intuition. It fosters awareness on many levels. Place it in the space when you meditate. Clear its energy after each use. Place in sun, a bowl of water, or salt. It loves to be outdoors, so be sure to cleanse and recharge it there.

Spirit Helpers

If you have a room or dedicated space in your home in which to meditate, you'll want to invite a calming and enlightened energy. Tara is an excellent choice. The goddess Tara brings a sense of calm and tranquility. She also functions as a protector and bringer of good luck. Many people revere her even today!

Meditation for Invoking the Energy of Tara

Create an environment for this meditation by lighting some beeswax or soy candles. Make sure the area is calm and quiet and you have a block of time to remain undisturbed. You might like to lie down for this, so use some pillows or cushions and make sure your body is super comfortable so you can go deep into this meditation.

The goddess Tara is considered a Buddha. A Buddha, also known as a bodhisattva in some traditions, is defined as someone who has attained a high level of wisdom and enlightenment while incarnated who often, then, ascended and in the case of Tara exists as a goddess who guides and assists people. She is a pinnacle of compassion, loving-kindness, and emptiness attained through deep meditation. She will help you meditate even more deeply and open your inner witness to greater enlightenment. She helps you live more mindfully and commit to a regular practice of meditation. You might even like to place an artist's depiction of her image or a symbol that reminds you of her in this space to help you live more presently and with a greater sense of peace.

Say the following affirmation aloud: "Dear Tara, please help me open my senses to my inner guidance and live more mindfully. I allow this awareness to enhance my health and well-being as well as my entire life. It is done." Then close your eyes and place your palms face up and connect with Tara and receive energy from her. Let this continue for as long as you choose and then say thank you and continue with your day.

Spirits of Place

Allow yourself to connect with the spirits who are responsible for the land over which your meditation area is built. Ask these beings to bring presence and mindful living to your life and being. State aloud in the meditation room, "I ask that all that transpires in this room be for the highest good of all life and in accordance with universal natural law, helping all, harming none. Please infuse this area with enhanced intuition and awareness of energy and all life." This will add an air of serenity and clarity to the place where you have your deepest thoughts.

Animal Helpers

The meditation room can be enhanced by the animal spirit of the mythical phoenix. This spirit activates your inner strength and resilience. The phoenix is a symbol of immortality and connection to the other side of the veil. This being touches the other side through rebirth amid the elemental force of fire. Let this energy activate you to live the life you desire and see clairvoyantly, hear clairaudiently, feel clairsentiently, and know claircognitively. Envision the phoenix soaring and flying over you imparting light and joy. You can say aloud, "I invoke the energy of the legendary phoenix to fill me with intuition, clarity, and power. Thank you for your presence, dear phoenix friends."

Cosmic Chimes Ritual

Use a set of chimes for this ritual. There are many kinds of chimes you could use. The handheld, circular cymbal-like chimes used in yoga classes are a great option for this ritual and can be used all around the house for space clearing. These are sometimes called Tibetan tingsha cymbals. You can use them to clear dense energy and then bring in stillness, intuition, and inspiration.

Begin in one corner of the room and chime vigorously. Start low and bring the cymbals up toward the ceiling. Then proceed to each corner, traveling in a clockwise direction. Open a window to picture density exiting, and then bend to the earth to recycle it back into pure white light. After chiming in each corner, do the same in the center of the room. After clearing your space, play the chimes more gently in the center of the room six times. In feng shui, six is the number that attracts and affirms helpful beings in your life. State aloud, "This room is infused with inspiration, spirit helpers and benevolent guides, intuition, and high-vibrational energy. I welcome the help of my benevolent, high-frequency guides and affirm my consent for them to intervene to help me create a life of joy, pleasure, comfort, ease, and living my heart's desires for my highest good. Thank you."

Sound
Clearing 101

You can use sound to clear your space any time you want! It is a tremendous way to remove dense energy from the home. Open windows when doing this to let the lower vibes out and send them back to the earth to be recycled into pure white light. You can use clapping hands, drums, musical instruments, rattles, your own voice, bells, shells that you blow through to make sound, or my favorite—a didgeridoo. Clear the corners, then the middle, then refill the space with high-vibe energy. One way to do that is to repeat the word *joy* over and over to fill the space with that energy. Joy is the highest vibrational energy in the known universe. Use it!

If you want, hop on to amyleighmercree.com/healinghomebookresources to get a space-clearing sound meditation to play in your house!

Feng Shui in the Meditation Room

The meditation room or area can be enhanced with a generous amount of emphasis on yin elements. Choose soft, natural fabrics, cushions, pillows, and velvety objects. To add a touch of yang, you can use shiny elements like satin fabrics to bring a bit of sheen that will keep energy moving. Use candles for warmth and plenty of soft lighting. Create a warm and inviting atmosphere to relax and allow yourself to quiet your mind and tune in to your inner being.

Feng Shui Meditation Room Cures

Because the space where you meditate is highly attuned to your spiritual frequency, these cures should be especially effective. Make sure you like how the energy in your space has changed after you place each one.

1. Practice a moving meditation in this room. By taking up space while in a meditative state, you will anchor mindful energy there.

2. The chi of this room should move slowly, but also be free flowing. Keep the space nice and clean and uncluttered so it can flow.

3. Use vertical elements to connect with the proverbial heavenly realms and elevate your perspective. Try tall plants or rounded sculptures with plenty of height.

4. Create an altarlike area of soulful focus. Place symbols that have meaning for you and connect you to that which is bigger than yourself and help you find the deeper meaning of life. Flowers are a wonderful addition here, too.

5. Use a D-note didgeridoo and create clearing sounds in the space regularly. The didge also activates your vagus nerve, stimulating the parasympathetic nervous system and inducing relaxation.

6. Create a spacious atmosphere with less clutter to open your mind to the world's possibilities.

7. Keep the energy in this room moving by turning on a fan when

you are not there. That way, when you enter, air has been moving and the energy will be fresh. Keep the air from any fans off of your body when you are in there. In excess, this wind energy can be disruptive to your liver chi.

8. Open the shades and windows to charge and freshen the energy in the room. Add a faceted feng shui crystal ball and hang it in the center of the room to keep everything flowing beautifully.

9. If you have released a bunch of energy in the room or it feels stagnant, place a bowl of sea salt in it overnight and empty the bowl outdoors the next day. The salt will have absorbed the stagnant and dense chi, which you can then give back to the earth.

> Refer back to The Elements section in the introduction and find out where in the bagua your meditation room is located and apply those cures to your room, too.

Vastu in the Meditation Room

Vastu is very focused on the spiritual and creating sanctuary. A meditation room is a wonderful place to be spiritual and invite in your creative essence. Meditation and spiritual exploration sometimes opens the door to flashes of insight and new ideas. And Vastu can help.

Vastu Meditation Room Cures

Here are some things you can do to use Vastu in the meditation room.

1. In Vastu, a puja (prayer) room is included in the layout of most homes. It is also known as the zone of tranquility in Vastu. It is a place to invite in positivity, clear your being, and relax deeply. This area can be its own room or a separate area in a particular room. It can even be a portable zone of tranquility such as a yoga mat that you unroll to let yourself move into serenity. Set up a tranquil space in whatever way works for your lifestyle.

2. Celebrate an aspect of nature in your zone of tranquility. Add your favorite natural elements from the world outside such as shells, stones, plants. Vastu invites us to bring nature into our spiritual practice and home.

3. Vastu tradition states that you should remove your shoes in the home and especially in the zone of tranquility to symbolically keep the denser elements of the outside world separate. Make sure you and your guests slip off your footwear before entering into the place where you'll be meditating.

CHAKRA HEALING IN THE MEDITATION ROOM

You can unleash the power of your chakras for healing your body in the meditation room. Read on to try some tips that can take your meditation area and presence to the next level.

Foot Chakras

The foot chakras are located in your feet and toes and are associated with communication and connection to the earth. Balanced foot chakras allow you to, as the saying goes, "walk the walk," rather than just "talking the talk." Use these chakras to help you be present in your spirituality and meditation to bring you into deeper mindfulness.

To open your foot chakra, consider integrating the crystal blue kyanite into your practice. It increases loyalty, which is perfect for your foot chakras. Often, people with blocked foot chakras have trouble with commitment. Kyanite, with its ability to encourage channeling, will help you stick to your plans and put the effort in to achieve your goals. Blue kyanite removes energy blockages, improves meditation practice, and works to align and balance all of your chakras together.

To balance your foot chakras, you'll need to break through the blocks caused by your anxieties. The essence of blue-bell flowers will dispel any fears you have that are preventing you from moving forward. Bluebell flowers have great healing powers and can lift your spirits on a dull or difficult day, opening you up to both divine and earthly energies.

Holistic Health Check

The meditation room benefits greatly from a low- or no-technology policy. Besides the obvious benefits of leaving a notification-plagued phone out of your space for clarity and contemplation, there are many studies that indicate that the blue light emitted by phone, tablets, and other devices can be harmful over the long term. Opt out of blue light as much as you can. You can use blue-light-blocking glasses for this purpose. TrueDark is one of several high-quality brands. You can wear these at night to create a feeling of deeper relaxation, even if you're not staring at your phone. Try them after dark when you meditate by candlelight with all tech devices off. They will lessen the impact of artificial light on your eyes, circadian rhythms, and body. Additionally, try wearing them for two hours before bed and notice how much better you sleep. Remember, they are only protecting your eyes from light, so you'll still want to limit your time in front of the screen, but they can mitigate the effects of a frequency that may be harmful to your eyesight.

CHAPTER 11

CHILDREN'S PLAYROOM

A playroom is a place where your children can unleash their imaginations and have fun. Fun is the essence of childhood! The recommendations contained within this chapter can be used for a play area even if it isn't an entire room. If your children are old enough to understand, you can have them help with the process of optimizing their spaces.

THE ENERGY OF THE PLAYROOM

Adding pleasant aromatherapy to their playroom made over the energy of Jen and Peter's children's playroom. They diffused some neroli essential oil in the room and removed most of the electronic toys and devices. They added lots of extra art supplies and more toys made with natural materials. They noticed their three children were getting along much better and playing more calmly even when simply making art or building structures by themselves.

AROMATHERAPY FOR THE PLAYROOM

Scents can be used to foster harmonious playtime and spark young minds. The right atmosphere can help kids think bigger and open their beings to greater expansion, which can lead to a more ease-filled, happy, and successful life. Use the harmonious scent of jasmine to bring agreeableness to the room. It will also calm them. Neroli essential oil will relax children and bring serenity. Lime essential oil enlivens the space and induces good health in children and adults alike.

THE WORLD IS YOUR PLAYROOM SPRITZ FOR KIDS

Use this easy linen spray to inspire kindness, empathy, and compassion.
It will help children become contributing, wonderful members of
society who think freely and care for others.
Kids may also enjoy helping prepare this recipe.

Ingredients

Spring or distilled water to almost fill the bottle of your choice
10 drops of neroli essential oil
10 drops of lime essential oil
5 drops of jasmine absolute essential oil

Place all the ingredients into a clean spray bottle and mix well.
Shake well before each use. You can spritz on furniture, carpets,
cushions, and stuffed toys, and if therapeutic-grade oils are used,
it's also a good scent to use topically.

Natural Toy Disinfectant Spray

Use this recipe to spray down toys to clean them without harsh chemicals. You can also use it on carpets, furniture, and pillows after someone has had a cold in place of chemical cleaning supplies that can damage your microbiome and cause respiratory problems.

Ingredients

Spring or distilled water to almost fill the bottle of your choice

20 to 30 drops of sage essential oil

20 to 30 drops of oregano
(or clove if you prefer that scent) essential oil

20 to 30 drops of thyme essential oil

20 to 30 drops of lemongrass essential oil

Place all the ingredients into a clean spray bottle and mix well.
Shake well before each use.

HOUSEPLANTS FOR THE PLAYROOM

Try sensitive plant in the playroom. Also known as *Mimosa pudica*, this tropical plant delights kids of all ages. This fun plant's leaves fold inward when they're touched. It needs warmth and all-day bright, indirect light. Place it near a corner of windows or on a windowsill and help your children learn to care for living things with regard and respect. It's a great plant to use for a teachable moment.

If you're looking for the right bloom to add to your kids' playroom, try fragrant lilacs of any color. They are symbols of confidence, exuberance, and joyful innocence. Their intoxicating aroma is both relaxing and enchanting, perfect for harmonious play and imaginative enjoyment. Show young children how to inhale and enjoy their aroma and appreciate their visual beauty and texture. Inspire mindful awareness of the magnificence of life and nature by modeling that behavior.

CRYSTALS FOR THE PLAYROOM

Children have a natural affinity for shiny stones and they may want to integrate these healing crystals into their play. Make sure these minerals are out of little ones' hands if they're likely to try to take a bite, but otherwise, let these gems be a gateway into greater interest in the power of crystals.

IRON PYRITE: This shiny, gold mineral is thought to be a stone of protection. It bounces negativity away so it can reduce fear and inspire secu-  rity in children. If your kiddo is shy and has a hard time getting along with new friends, place pyrite in the room before a playdate.

LAPIS LAZULI: The rich, electric blue of this stone attracts children. It can help support healthy expression of intuitive gifts in children and stabilize those gifts. If painting or drawing is a big activity in your kids' playroom, this is an excellent stone to have nearby.

SPIRIT HELPERS

It can be hard to leave your kids alone to play, so it's never a bad idea to call upon the energies of a protector deity when you'd like someone to watch over them in your absence. Alternatively, perhaps you'd like a little more help when children are wild or are having a frustrating school experience that even you can't seem to fix. Benzaiten, also known as Benten, is a Japanese water goddess known as a protector of children. She can also help children with learning because she is a patroness of learning letters, language, and words, as well as poetry. She is also benefactress of the arts, music, and overall learning and curiosity. In Japan, she is famed for being one of the seven lucky deities.

Meditation to Invoke the Energy of Benten

To call upon the energy of Benten and all of her gifts, consider the following meditation. Tap into her benevolence for you and your children by saying the following invocation aloud: "Dear Benzaiten, please create a space of physical safety and emotional security in this room and house. Please protect all who live here and dispel all that is not for the highest good. Please invite a sense of blissful enjoyment of life and learning here for all. Stoke creativity and intelligence and help us all partake of the fun and richness of life. Thank you!"

Spirits of Place

Call in the spirits who govern the land over which your kids' playroom or area is built. Ask them to infuse the room with joy and creativity. Intend that the space will expand your children's minds, hearts, spirits, and souls. Imagine your children receiving whatever they need from this space with ease and happiness. See your children having a space to be kids and detach from the pressures of modern life. Envision that they can experience their imaginations and downgrade their nervous systems here for optimum health. You and/or your child or children can state the following aloud in the room: "I ask that all that transpires in this room be for the highest good of all life and in accordance with universal natural law, helping all, harming none. Please bring joy and bliss into this space and align us all with a beautiful life full of ease, pleasure, prosperity, and creative exuberance."

Animal Helpers

Children can participate in this visualization. What a fun way to ignite the flames of imagination. We will connect with the guardian spirit of an animal helper for your playroom. Envision a blue jay or scrub jay. They look very similar, but the blue jay has a crest on the top of the head. Both are beautiful blue-and-white birds with eye-catching feathers and tails.

All jays are highly intelligent, playful, and exuberant. Scrub jays are the only animal besides people who plan ahead for the future. Studies found that they plan what kind of food they will eat for breakfast the next morning and how much. They gather it the day before and store away the right amount for later.

Picture a beautiful jay with splendid, colorful feathers hopping lightly across the room. Allow the idea of an animal guardian to stoke your imagination. You, and/or your child can say aloud: "I welcome the jubilant spirit of the intelligent jay to enliven this room with curiosity, creativity, and fun. Thank you for your presence, dear friend."

Peppermint Playroom Ritual

Peppermint is the perfect plant for the playroom. It is full of vivifying qualities and energizing botanicals. It also promotes clear thinking and decisive, correct action. We want our children to feel empowered and confident, and to enjoy life. This plant brings all of that into being with its botanical and energetic properties.

Befriend the plants that help you! You eat them. You smell them. You enjoy their benefits for healing. Plants are our friends. Teach kids who are receptive this important understanding. Respecting and caring for plants as living beings teaches empathy and an appreciation of nature.

Befriend the peppermint plant in whatever way you are able. If you have a garden or container garden, you can plant this botanical and children can help and learn how to water and care for the plants. If not, you can obtain fresh peppermint at the store, on a plant or just the leaves. In all cases, organic is recommended.

Teach children to gather the leaves of mint and rinse them gently and then eat a few fresh, then sprinkle them on salads or berries or add them to a fun mocktail. Try one made with sparkling water, lime juice, a few muddled strawberries, and some mint leaves for a strawberry mint delight. You can add a tiny dash of organic powdered stevia to taste if desired. It's fun for kids to learn how food comes from nature.

Next, you can dry some mint for later by hanging the stems, with leaves still attached, upside down tied with a cotton string. Leave for a week or so and check the progress with the kids. Consider hanging them low enough so children can touch and inspect them without help.

Take some fresh mint leaves on the stem and place them in a heat-safe vessel. Some people use an abalone shell, or you can use a stainless steel bowl placed on a trivet or silicone mat made for high heat. Place the mint in its vessel in the playroom and open the windows. Have oven mitts handy. Use a long match or grill lighter to light the fresh mint.

Make sure to carefully monitor the flames, and if children are present, never leave them unsupervised or let them be too close to the fire. Warn children of the risk of fire and store all matches and lighters up high. Blow out the flames after a few moments so the smoldering mint emits a gentle stream of smoke. You may choose to carefully hold the bowl with the oven mitt and slowly move around the room, "sprinkling" the smoke throughout. Be careful to avoid flammable surfaces and fabrics like curtains.

Say out loud: "I [or *we* if your child is there] invite prosperous, jubilant, and high-vibrational energy to fill this room with happiness and bliss for the very highest good of all life. That which is of the light fills this room." Waft the smoke through the room. Monitor the embers and make sure they burn out completely. Make sure the bowl and burned mint are totally cool before handling. Do not leave the flames or embers unwatched and have a fire extinguisher handy for safety. After the ritual is complete, keep windows and doors open to allow even more fresh energy to fill the space.

After the mint is dried, you can use the above process and notice the similarities and differences when fresh or dried mint is burned. Invite children to compare both aromas. They will both be pleasant and enlivening!

Feng Shui in the Playroom

The playroom should be a place for kids to have fun, learn, enjoy life, and unleash their imaginations. Its energy should change according to the optimal level of stimulation for their ages, so that as kids get older their own tastes and preferences are represented. Try involving kids in the arrangement of the space, because it may make a huge difference for them.

About 20 percent of the population are *highly sensitive people* or HSPs. These people have more sensitive nervous systems, and this trait is innate and inherited. This research was pioneered by Dr. Elaine Aron, and her books are excellent resources if you think you or your child is an HSP. If you think your child may be a highly sensitive person, help them create environments in the home where they can escape sensory overwhelm, so they can better manage the stimulation they encounter in the world outside. HSPs tend to prefer some extra yin elements like soft lighting and fabrics and more quiet areas. Excessive yang in the home can overwhelm an HSP.

The playroom is well served with a mix of yin and yang. Depending on the child, anywhere from about 60 percent yin and 40 percent yang to 90 percent yin and 10 percent yang will be the right balance.

Feng Shui Playroom Cures

Here are a few tips for creating that balance between yin and yang and making a few other changes that will work with the energies of the bagua:

1. If more than one child lives at home and the playroom is shared, help children find the balance of yin and yang they prefer. If one child is in need of a cozy, soft space for quiet play and the other wants to be loud and active, consider setting times for both active and introspective activities. Encourage the child whose preferred energy is not in the playroom to go to a bedroom or outdoors.

2. Help kids define what makes them feel relaxed and joyful. Ask questions like, "What amount of light feels good for drawing?" "When you are reading, do you like it to be quiet, or does music in the background help you enjoy your book?" Help children add soft lamps and throw blankets and add or subtract sound depending on what they are doing and how they are feeling. Teaching children how to self-regulate in this way is an important life skill and creates stress management skills for adulthood.

3. Would your child enjoy a dedicated Lego or art area? Does he or she dream of a drum set? Ask and try to provide elements that will inspire them to explore more of who they are. Perhaps a full drum set isn't in the cards, but maybe a handful of percussive instruments would fill the need for rhythm and sound. These elements will keep the chi of the room fresh and flowing, that's for sure!

4. Eschew televisions in this room. Teach children to enjoy tangible play from an early age. They will make more dendritic connections and develop more useful skills for life if they are curious and mentally sharp. If you do want to have a television in the space, consider placing it in a cabinet out of view so it is not the first thing kids go to for entertainment when they enter.

5. Warm colors bring a touch of yang and life to the room. Consider yellows, oranges, and pinks of any shade to invoke sunshine in the space. Cool tones will promote a relaxed atmosphere, so if your children gravitate toward calm and quiet, listen and allow them to enjoy what feels good and honor their senses.

6. Create an area for children to display their art that is not merit

based. Simply allow it to be a place for them to share their creativity and encourage them to enjoy seeing it when they enter.

7. Shades of the color white, circles, metal, and shiny silver elements foster creativity. If your playroom is a heavy art, music, dance, or creative zone, add these elements. For example, a silver round metal trash bin can be added with intention to enrich the artistic chi in the space.

8. To encourage growth, use columnar elements, wood furniture and decorations, and the color green as well as live plants. All of these cures that add wood element energy promote new, fresh perspectives and are in harmony with children and their stage of life. Think growing trees, plants, leaf and flower prints, lush vegetation, and columnar bamboo.

9. Teens are entering a stage of life that moves from the wood element to the fire element. Preteens feel influences of both in their beings. Help kids who are experiencing these ages add accents of the fire element with stronger colors, tall triangular shapes, and even animal prints. However, a little goes a long way, so be careful not to make the space too overstimulating.

The Cycle of the Elements

The Taoist creative cycle begins with wood and ends with water. Then, water becomes wood and the cycle begins again, ever renewing.

WOOD

Spring

Birth

Green

Columnar, vertical

East

FIRE

Summer

Growth

Red

Triangular, vertical

South

EARTH

Late Summer

Transformation

Yellow

Square, horizontal

Middle

METAL

Autumn

Harvest

White

Circular

West

WATER

Winter

Storing

Black

Formless, endless, undulating

North

Vastu in the Playroom

Vastu will help you create a sanctuary for your children in their playroom. This way, they have a special space to open their minds and hearts through imagination.

> Refer back to The Elements section in the introduction and find out where in the bagua your playroom is located and *gently* apply those cures to the room.
> Go easy so as not to overwhelm your children energetically.

Vastu Playroom Cures

Use these tips to add the healing of Vastu to the playroom:

1. Vastu is all about harmonizing your environment with nature. Bring nature inside the playroom by allowing children to collect rocks, shells, sticks, and other clean outdoor nature items and display them creatively. Try a fun art project using these materials.

2. Teach children to seek harmony in their environment in the spirit of Vastu. Help them think this through as you arrange how their toys are stored. Consider using large, natural fiber baskets or light, wooden slatted boxes. Ask kids to consider what shapes resonate for them: do they like round or square shapes more? Think together about where in nature we see round versus square shapes.

3. In Vastu, your child's playroom is meant help them to feel like an important part of the family. With your child, pick out a couple favorite family photographs to display there.

CHAKRA HEALING IN THE PLAYROOM

Optimize the root chakra and enliven the playroom. This will bring vitality and positive energy to your children's lives.

Root Chakra

The root chakra is located at the base of your spine and is associated with being grounded and feeling stable. It impacts your feelings of stability and security.

Obsidian is a good stone for opening the root chakra, because its energy is very stabilizing. Obsidian forms when lava cools and hardens into shiny black stones. It is known for being a "guardian stone" that protects you both physically and metaphysically from negative energies. It contains many earthly properties that will resonate with the root chakra and leave your children feeling confi-

dent and strong. Obsidian is thought to have many physical benefits, including fighting viral infections and improving the health of the stomach and muscle tissue.

When you want to balance the root chakra, consider working with dandelion. It is an adaptable plant that you often see growing in cracks and peppering lawns with color and sunshine. These types of plants help adapt to all kinds of stressors, including temperature extremes, loud noises, changes in altitude, and changing schedules. They promote endurance and strength, so they are an ideal choice for grounding. These flowers are also fun for children to gather and place in bud vases in the playroom, and readily available for picking in many yards. Being in contact with the plant and its adaptable energy will benefit children in numerous ways, and it is another way to foster appreciation of the outdoor environment.

ADAPTABLE PLANTS, AKA ADAPTOGENS

Adaptogens are herbs and plants that help us adapt to environmental stressors. Dandelion is an herbal adaptogen just like holy basil (tulsi), ginseng,

ginger, turmeric, ashwagandha, and Rhodiola. Adults can enjoy these powerhouses in teas for adrenal support, to promote a healthy immune system, and for a host of other reasons.

HOLISTIC HEALTH CHECK

Check the playroom for toxic hazards. Aim for pure cotton or linen for optimum health including cushions, carpets, clothing, bedding, and curtains. Choose wood, metal, and fabric—not plastic—for toys if possible. By minimizing the amount of plastics with which your children come into contact, you also limit their exposure to harmful chemical additives that are sometimes present in these materials. Find natural alternatives for better health and well-being.

PART 5

CLEARING, HOLDING & MOVEMENT

*I*n this section, we will talk about the places that your friends and family pass through; those that contain the most movement in the home as well as those that are primarily storage areas. The bathrooms and laundry room are crucial areas—places of clearing and flowing water. They are where we lighten our bodies, clean, and move energy in numerous ways. We will discuss how to clear the old and invite the fresh and new in the home by harnessing the power of these spaces. Let's dive in!

CHAPTER 12

BATHROOM

Bathrooms are places of flowing and moving energy and water. They are where we collect ourselves for the upcoming day and unwind after it is complete. We will take a look at how to optimize the main bathroom as well as half baths, children's bathrooms, and guest bathrooms.

THE ENERGY OF THE BATHROOM

When the bathroom is filled with light and life, it sets the stage for beautiful day. Stacy cleared out all of her old makeup and toiletries as well as having a broken exhaust fan fixed. She added some lovely plants and favorite aromatherapy elements and found her days were better because she began her morning in a positive state of mind.

AROMATHERAPY IN THE BATHROOM

Use the power of scent in the bathroom to evoke a sense of well-being and foster good health. Lemongrass is the perfect scent for the bathrooms. It has a clean and refreshing countenance and offers a simultaneously relaxing essence. Fun fact: it is also helpful for "texting thumb" when applied topically to the affected area. For a relaxing (or romantic) bath ritual, you can use ylang-ylang, lavender, gardenia, jasmine, rose, vanilla, and cocoa essential oils—they're all good for setting the mood.

SHOWER AROMATHERAPY

Wet a washcloth and place a few drops of your favorite essential oils on it, then hang it over the shower head out of the way of the water to let the steam of the shower diffuse the scent for you.

CLEAN AND CLEAR BATHROOM SPRITZ

Use this aromatherapy spray to impart a sense of freshness. You can also use it on your body as a clean, light perfume!

Ingredients

Spring or distilled water to almost fill the bottle of your choice

15 drops of lemongrass essential oil
10 drops of lemon essential oil
5 drops of grapefruit essential oil

Place all the ingredients into a clean spray bottle and mix well. Shake well before each use. You can spritz your countertops, shower walls, sinks, faucets, towels, and washcloths.

HOUSEPLANT FOR THE BATHROOM

The Chinese evergreen houseplant brings living chi into the bathroom. Also known as Aglaonema, this plant is a tropical perennial with large leaves that adds an air of lushness and beauty to what can be a utilitarian space. They enjoy humidity, so they're also a good candidate for a steamy bathroom. They can tolerate dry air, but not cold breezes, so keep your plant away from a direct air-conditioning vent, though. They do well in low, indirect light and do not like direct sunlight.

Flowers impart light and energy to the bathroom. Euphrasia is a lovely flower with delicate blooms of light purple with yellow markings. Display them in the bathrooms that are used frequently. This plant being helps people make decisions and increases intuition. I like to keep some near the shower because it is a natural place to feel intuitive hunches. Eufrasia will magnify this tendency—if you've ever had a "eureka!" moment in the shower and

want it to happen more often, this flower is the one to pick. Euphrasia is a helpful friend and spirit in the body of a flower. Make sure you thank it!

CRYSTALS FOR THE BATHROOM

Many people won't think of the bathroom as a place to linger, but if you add beautiful accents like the crystals that follow, you can give it the energy it needs to be a sanctuary during a busy day, a calming place for a moment of peace. Add a little luxury and serenity to your bath routine with these stones:

LARIMAR: A gorgeous stone infused with the essence of the ocean and, some even think, the energy of dolphins, larimar is harmonious with the water element and amplifies its positive effects.

ROSE QUARTZ: This stone anchors unconditional love and acceptance in the bathroom, a place where people relax and unwind as well as allow themselves to experience self-care. The energy imparted—a bit of unconditional self-acceptance—is a gift to give yourself and your family every time anyone enters. This stone can join you in a bath ritual and be immersed in water with you. Just be sure to put it outside after for a few days so it can decompress and recharge in the sun and moonlight.

Spirit Helpers

Cleanliness is said to be next to godliness—it's true that feeling refreshed is divine. To add a bit of that otherworldly feeling of clarity, consider invoking the Greek and Roman goddess of health, Hygieia. She is a force of vitality and cleanliness. She can help us clean up energy as well as physicality. She teaches us how to properly care for our unique bodies. Every

body, mind, and spirit are unique, and it's important to remember that what works for one person may have a different effect on another. Hygieia can help you to know yourself and tap into that which is for your highest and most healthful good.

Hygieia is known to prevent sickness. Call on her to infuse your home with good health and the insight checking in with your body requires. The energy of Hygieia can create healing, physical ease, and comfort by helping you recognize your unique needs. Invite the energy of this goddess into your life and receive her favor with gratitude.

Meditation to Invoke Hygieia

State the following invocation aloud in the bathroom you use the most: "Dear Hygieia, please help me to experience perfect health and complete ease, comfort, and frequent pleasure and joy in my body. Thank you. It is done."

Hygieia has come to you today to help you let go of anything limiting your full enjoyment of the life and experience of complete and total health. If you choose, tell Hygieia, "Yes," and she will clear you of dense energy and patterns of thinking that no longer serve you. She will replace these with habits that promote health and thinking that are proactive and positive to create a healthy cellular environment and to infuse your internal organs with true health and light energy. You can accept this gift. Hygieia is truly happy to help you. It allows her to be in service and share her gifts. It is a win-win situation. Accept the kindness and generosity of this goddess and receive the beauty of life with joy and gratitude. Life is meant to be easy. You are meant to be healthy, and your body is an amazing self-regulating and self-correcting wonder.

Spirits of Place

Call in the spirits that govern the land over which your bathroom is built. Ask them for clarity and healthful high-vibrational energy. State aloud in the bathroom, "I ask that all that transpires in this room be for the highest good of all life and in accordance with universal natural law, helping all, harming none.

Please bring vibrant high-frequency light into this space and clear the energy of this space to allow for sparkling health and effervescent vitality.

Animal Helpers

Connect with a guardian spirit of an animal helper for the bathrooms in your home. Feel the sweet and generous spirit of the honeybee in your heart. Imagine calm, happy honeybees in a hive buzzing with productivity and community. These bees have no interest in stinging or coming too close to you—they simply hold space for sweet enjoyment and productivity and share it with you. Cross-culturally, bees have been known as powerful shamanic allies. Perhaps they will provide their magic for you and your household, too. Allow the splendid idea of an animal guardian to delight your imagination. Picture the bees buzzing about, creating honey and royal jelly as a collective team. You can say aloud, "I welcome the benevolent spirit of the honeybee, who is here to sweeten this room with light and health. Thank you for your presence, dear friend."

LEMONGRASS BATHROOM BURN RITUAL

This lemongrass burning ritual is a form of smoke clearing. Smoke clearing is practiced all over the world in many cultures. In this case, you are adding the energy of the lemongrass plant to your space and simultaneously removing unwanted energy. You are catalyzing the dried, organic lemongrass with the fire element and releasing it into the environment in a potent manner. Lemongrass promotes clarity and vibrancy. It enlivens a space and brings light and high-vibrational energy. It also has clearing properties and loosens and transmutes dense energy to make space for more light.

Materials

Heatproof bowl or dish

Dried lemongrass (stalks or loose herbs)
Long wooden match or long grill lighter
Trivet or silicone mat and/or thick pot holder or oven mitt

Place the lemongrass in the bowl.
Place the trivet or silicone mat in the room. Set the bowl on top of it.
Keep the bowl away from anything flammable like fabric and carpeting.
Make sure there's an open area around the bowl so it will not cause

an unintended fire. Light the herb and allow the flames to burn for a moment before blowing them out, so that the smoldering herb emits a consistent stream of smoke. You may choose to carefully hold the bowl with the oven mitt and slowly move around the room, "sprinkling" the smoke throughout. Again, be careful to avoid flammable surfaces and fabrics like curtains.

State, "I now clear all density from this space and fill it with high-vibrational energy for the very highest good of all life. Only that which is of the light fills this room." Waft the smoke through the room. Watch the fire burn out completely. Make sure the bowl and material are totally cool before handling, and never leave the flames or embers unwatched. Have a fire extinguisher handy for safety. After the ritual is complete, open the windows and doors to allow even more fresh energy to fill the space.

FENG SHUI IN THE BATHROOM

Bathrooms should be mostly energetically yang. Think smooth, shiny surfaces and clean expanses of space. You can add a dash of health-promoting yin by choosing rounded edges and corners over sharpness. Have some yin and yang lighting options available: some softer and some more bright and direct.

Feng Shui Bathroom Cures

State your intentions for the bathroom aloud as you place some of the cures below. You'll notice the effects right away in some cases—try one, then gradually add more if you would like.

1. Candles in the main bathroom are a lovely way to bring warmth to a generally cool energy area.
2. In Traditional Chinese Medicine, the kidneys, which are water element organs, are called the palaces of fires and water. Think about this in the bathroom. Represent the water element via the faucets and add a bit of fire element through a candle or warm lighting element. Use intention in placing all of your cures and envision your kidneys receiving the exact energy they need to be healthy and feel how your home supports that. Enjoy a cup of kidney-regulating raspberry leaf tea in a warm bath to show your kidneys some love.
3. White is often present in the bathroom, and there is a reason for that: it is a wonderful aid when you are seeking new directions or want to reduce procrastination. Use intention and place your hand on a white part of the room and say aloud what you want in positive affirmative terms. Harness the power of your existing decor.
4. Keep toilet seats down when flushing and when not in use to prevent energetic drains. Plus, it looks better and nothing will accidentally fall in!

5. Use upward-facing elements and decor in the bathroom to move the energy up from the downward pull of the toilets and drains. Crown molding does this as well as decorative elements placed higher on the wall, like painted borders.

6. Prevent actual dampness, which produces damp energy. In TCM (Traditional Chinese Medicine), we call this "damp accumulation," and it can happen in organs and meridians in addition to physical spaces like rooms (and if it's present in rooms, it can find its way to your organs). By eschewing dampness in your environment, you can balance your body. While moisture is totally healthy and wonderful when you are bathing, it's not great to keep hanging around in the bathroom for hours afterward. It is a great idea to keep the area well ventilated especially after showers. Check for leaks under the all the sinks in the house. They create stagnant water chi and must be fixed as soon as possible. Dripping faucets also require immediate fixing so as not promote leaky, damp energy.

7. Avoid fabrics in the bathroom besides towels. They create stagnancy and hold moisture. Choose materials that diminish humidity.

8. Plants will absorb humidity, so place them liberally in the bathroom.

9. Wooden blinds are preferred in the bathroom over curtains. Choose slatted blinds so some sunlight can come in and you can still have

privacy. Make sure to raise the blinds daily and let in the sunlight. Open the windows daily, if possible, to bring fresh air and chi into the room and release trapped energy.

> Refer back to The Elements section in the introduction and find out where in the bagua your bathrooms are located and apply those cures to your room, too.

Vastu in the Bathroom

Vastu places much emphasis on hygiene and so it is helpful in all of the bathrooms of the home. It can be used to enhance these areas with intention and thoughtfulness.

Vastu Bathroom Cures

Here are some ways you can use Vastu in the bathroom:

1. In the Vastu tradition, medicines and supplements that are in the bathroom are best kept on the northern wall, where they receive the blessing of the deity Soma. Soma is considered the lord of health. If keeping your medications on the northern wall is not possible, just use intention to ask for Soma to grant beneficence to you and your family as well as the medicines and supplements wherever they are kept.

2. Taking a bath is often a sacred ritual, and Vastu has plenty of wisdom relative to addressing the spiritual side of bathing. In Vastu, the bathroom is considered a spiritual place for connecting to the divine, as well as your intuition. In this space, you cleanse the body that temporally houses your sacred soul until someday you return to a nonphysical form. Think about bathing as an opportunity to pamper your body, which houses your soul, the all-important vehicle of your truth in Vastu. Embrace this tradition and make self-care and bath time a priority.

3. Vastu often emphasizes bringing nature into the home. Consider

adding medicinal plants to your bathroom, if possible: aloe vera, mint, lavender, rosemary. You can add these plants to your bath-time rituals, and they'll add beauty to the space.

Chakra Healing in the Bathroom

You can heal your chakras and bathrooms using complementary strategies. Paying attention to your chakras can help you create a healthy body and environment in your home.

Sacral Chakra

The sacral chakra is located in the lower abdomen, and is associated with creativity, sexuality, and reproduction. It is part of the process of digesting and releasing old energy and ancestral

patterns—perfect for the literal, as well as the figurative, aspects of the bathroom.

To open the sacral chakra, consider integrating the mineral jasper into your practice. All varieties of jasper are grounding, and yellow jasper is especially good for this purpose. The biggest plus when it comes to this stone is that it gives you a renewed sense of optimism. It works at a deeper level to bring more positive things into your life. It helps to reduce stress and will leave you feeling happier. Charge it in the sun to enhance its positive aspects.

For balancing the sacral chakra, you might consider using the herb damiana. Damiana has been used throughout history, from ancient civilizations up until today. It has many effects that can promote feelings of happiness, joy, and euphoria. It is known for its antidepressant and aphrodisiac qualities. You can consume it by drying the leaves of the herb and then infusing the leaves to make a tea or a steam for inhalation. Inhalation of this herb's vapors in large quantities has been reported to produce more intense feelings of euphoria. Overall, it promotes feelings of comfort and joy. Drink a tea of dried damiana or add its leaves to the water in your tub for a resplendent bath.

Holistic Health Check

Make sure to switch all of your toiletries and cleaning products to those without VOCs and other harmful chemicals. Choose products with ingredients that are simple and either aren't scented or have fragrances derived from essential oils. Skip the phthalates and parabens. Check out resources from the Environmental Working Group at *ewg.org* to learn how products rate. Replace conventional soaps with goat's milk and natural-ingredient, organic soaps made with things like almond oil and coconut oil. Look for shampoos and conditioners made with ingredients you recognize and can pronounce and eschew all of the problematic ingredients like ammonium lauryl sulfate (ALS) or sodium laureth sulfate (SLES) as well as sodium lauryl sulfate (SLS), sodium chloride, polyethylene glycols (PEG), formaldehyde, alcohol, and synthetic fragrances. Check makeup for the following harmful ingredients: fragrance, triclosan, formaldehyde-releasing preservatives, sodium laureth sulfate, retinyl palmitate, retinyl acetate, retinoic acid and retinol, and petroleum distillates.

CHAPTER 13

TRANSITIONAL SPACES

TRANSITIONAL SPACES

*I*n this section we are going to look at spaces like hallways, laundry rooms, basements, and attics. We will make these areas healthy and help their energy support you and your family.

LAUNDRY ROOM

The laundry room (or area) is a place where we clean our clothing and is another important area of moving and clearing. We take our fabric (yin) items, which are prone to holding energy, and use movement and water to remove dirt and oils as well as energetic density. To keep the energy in this space moving and flowing, choose shiny surfaces, clutter-free expanses, and no extra fabric (like curtains). Just as in bathrooms, we want to eschew dampness and prevent moisture and humidity from accumulating in the space. The only fabrics needed in the laundry are the ones being cleaned. Be vigilant about leaks and stagnant water chi by checking frequently and having necessary repairs made immediately.

Use scent from essential oils liberally in this space. Keep some favorites in the room and toss a few drops in the dryer with each load to scent your items and the room. Here are some great options to try:

Clary sage

Grapefruit

Cardamom

Bergamot

Nutmeg

Lavender

Geranium

Sandalwood

Fir

Sweet marjoram

Peppermint

Fennel

Tangerine

Sweet orange

(note: don't use sweet orange if you have a tendency toward migraines or headaches, as this can be a trigger)

Make sure to choose nontoxic chemicals here, too. No VOCs or other harmful chemicals. Switch out your laundry detergents and make sure they are only scented with essential oils, not "fragrance." Skip fabric softeners for ecofriendly wool dryer balls you can scent with essential oils. If you'd like, go to amyleighmercree.com/healinghomebookresources for easy, printable recipes for my nontoxic DIY Laundry Detergent and DIY Fabric Freshener (healthy fabric softener replacement).

Laundry Room Lavender Refresh Ritual

To create a fragrant haven, hang some fresh lavender upside down and tied with a cotton string in the laundry area. After it has dried, you can take some stems out and place them in a heat-safe vessel. Some people use an abalone shell, or you can use a stainless-steel bowl placed on a trivet or silicone mat made for high heat. Place the dried sprigs in the vessel and open any windows and doors. Have oven mitts handy. Use a long match or grill lighter to light the lavender. Let the flames burn for a moment, then blow them out so the smoldering herb emits a gentle stream of smoke. You may choose to carefully hold the bowl with the oven mitt and slowly move around the room, "sprinkling" the smoke throughout. Please be careful to avoid flammable surfaces and fabrics.

Say out loud: "I invite this space to easily clear density from our clothing and home and ask that a constant flow of high-vibrational energy fill this space with joy and vitality for the very highest good of all life. That which is of the light fills this room." Waft the smoke through the room. Watch as the herb burns completely. Make sure the bowl and material are totally cool before handling, and do not leave the flames or embers unwatched. Have a fire extinguisher handy for safety. After this ritual is complete, keep the windows and doors open to allow even more fresh energy to fill the space.

HALLWAY

Hallways are transitional spaces, and the chi there needs to be kept moving freely. Debris, dust, and especially clutter will oversaturate the area with density and impede the flow of chi. It is so important to clear your spaces. Free-flowing energy in transitional spaces allows for new opportunities to enter.

You can place bowls of sea salt in hallways to absorb any dense energy. Add a drop of your favorite essential oil if you'd like to add scent. Leave sea salt overnight and then empty outside, if possible, to give the dense energy absorbed back to the earth and recycle it into pure, white light.

Super-long hallways accelerate chi in a major way. This can be great if you'd like to amplify energy, but if opportunities feel like they are rushing by you and impossible to grab, you can add a rug to cushion their path so you can access them more easily.

CHAPTER 14

SPACES FOR STORAGE

*I*n this section, we will tap into the foundational energy of the home to make sure that we are setting a powerful stage to create the life of your dreams. As you know, your home's energy is so important when it comes to setting the stage for the dreams of your future. That includes storage areas where friends and family don't necessarily congregate. We will expand the strength of energy in the areas that hold chi, such as the basement, garage, closets, and attic, and make sure they support the frequency of your home aligned with your desired frequency for life.

BASEMENT

Keep the basement door closed so it doesn't drain chi down and out of the house. Minimize the arrow energy of stair railings down to the basement. They create an additional energy drain.

Paint the railings, stairs, and walls a light color like off-white or very light gray to act in a less absorbent manner and to also symbolically disguise and minimize that downward pull.

ATTIC

Dried clove can be burned safely to dispel negative or stagnant energy in the attic. And, as always, a good cleaning and clearing of clutter and dust is a major chi refresher. If anything is mentally hanging over your head, this will clear it away.

CLOSETS

The closets that hold clothing are associated with identity and personality. They hold the chi and fabric that partially represent to the outside world what is on the inside. If you want to enhance your image, clean your closet! Leave some space open in the closet to allow for new, fresh energy into your life. Purge clothing that doesn't fit or look wonderful and make you feel good and like who you want to be.

GARAGE

Garages accumulate clutter and, as we know, clutter is an energy stagnator. Organize it. Minimize it. And sweep it frequently to keep the chi fresh and moving.

CHAPTER 15

OUTDOOR AREAS

Your home doesn't begin and end inside the walls of the house. Your yard or outdoor area also plays a part in the energetic frequency to which your living space is attuned, and this includes your porch, balcony, and patio. In this chapter, we will set the stage for your home with the yard and surroundings. Your environment on the outside attracts great energy into the home.

THE ENERGY OF THE OUTDOOR AREAS

Consider what chi you need more of in the home. Yin energy can be magnetized if you use wooden materials for the balcony and by adding soft, fluffy vegetation to trellises. Consider growing vines with flowers in delicate colors that evoke feminine energy. If you are in need of yang in the home, choose plants with strong colors or spiked leaves and containers with a yang vibe made with shiny and strong materials. Plastic pots and containers disrupt the chi of the home, so try to use natural materials.

Invoking the Energy of the Green Man in Your Outdoor Areas

Invite the Green Man onto your patio, balcony, or porch—or really, any outdoor area! Who is the Green Man, you ask? This being is a guide who brings wild, nourishing nature to your door. A Celtic mythological figure known for supporting growth and helping you get in touch with your healthy, primal nature, the Green Man is a benevolent being who can also stoke the flames of libido and bring balance and fire to the divine masculine within us all. Head outside and state aloud, "Dearest Green Man, I invite you to bring the magic of nature to my home. I am so grateful for your high-vibrational help for my highest good and the highest good of all life and in accordance with universal natural law. Please invoke abundance, prosperity, and wealth to this home and infuse it with passion and joy." Close your eyes for a few moments and let yourself feel aromatic breezes and sense the smell of fresh soil. Allow yourself to feel the essence of the Green Man.

TIPS FOR POOL AREA, DRIVEWAY, AND YARD

» Pull out the salt, a powerful energetic tool in an unassuming package, and sprinkle a little bit of it around the perimeter of your property while stating, "This salt shall screen out density and attract joy and wealth to this home for the highest good. It is done."

» Windchimes are the ticket if you want to call in money. Metal is a symbol of coins and wealth, so metal windchimes are key for this purpose—their long, hollow columnar rods hold money chi for you! Hang chimes by the front door to call wealth into your life.

» Invoke the energy of the Irish goddess Danu to boost the health of your yard. She will bring romance, love, beauty, prosperity, and understanding to your life. She can foster ease and comfort. Call her in while sitting or lying down outside in your yard. Quiet your mind and calm your thoughts. Breathe deeply by inhaling for three seconds and then exhaling for five. Do that ten times to activate your parasympathetic nervous system, which is your rest-and-digest, relaxed state. Being able to enter this state is paramount for stress relief, and it's also the right state of mind to be in if you want to listen to your spirit guides. State aloud, "Dearest Danu, please come enchant this yard with your splendor and light. Open my eyes to the magnificence of life and the beauty of nature. Please enchant our life and draw high-vibrational energy to this yard and home. Thank you so much for your love and favor. I am grateful and joyful." Then, continue breathing and feel Danu all around you. Let yourself feel her presence. Place your hands out in front of your body, palms up. Invite Danu to hover her spirit hands over yours. Sink into the feeling and notice whether your hands get warm, tingle, or feel like they are pulsing. Stay that way and commune with Danu. When the process feels complete, say "thank you."

» Add a nice, large boulder to the yard, preferably the backyard. It will anchor the space's chi and provide stable mountain energy to back you up when you try new things and make important decisions.

» Remove dead leaves from the property and gutters. They hold stagnant, dead chi.

» When you plant a cluster of new flowers outside, the togetherness and clustering can call in new opportunities. You may have renewed success if you've been trying to network, or you

may find that friends or colleagues will reach out with job offers or ideas for collaboration. Plant these clusters of flowers with intention, stating what you want to call in. For example, "This cluster of flowers brings me fun networking opportunities that create financial windfalls and knowledge about how to invest for optimal outcomes."

» Studies show that smelling soil—specifically its microbe *M. vaccae*—boosts serotonin and norepinephrine. It is similar in effect to antidepressant pills. This organic compound is sometimes called *geosmin* by scientists. That dirt smell gives carrots and beets their earthy taste. If you want to improve family relations and other relationships, including romantic, then digging in the garden together can incite good feelings, which allows for bonding.

» No thorny plants by the front door, please. You want to invite good energy in, and thorns will repel it.

» Plant succulents in the yard to hold water energy. Water energy equals money energy.

» Trees in the backyard, not too close to the house, will lend support to its inhabitants. Trees are living guardians, your supporters and cheerleaders. Keep them alive and healthy and remember to connect with them and thank them for their support. If trees or vegetation are too close to the house, they smother and stagnate the energy, so keep everything nice and pruned and keep vines off the house.

» Place a birdbath in the yard close to the front door to gather water and bring in prosperity. Keep it relatively close to the front door so it can bring that resonant water chi inside easily.

» If you want to invite energy, leave the outside lights on for a minimum of three hours per night.

» If you make sure your address is visible on your home or mailbox, then new opportunities can find you. Freshen it up!

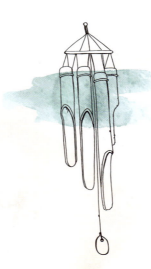

YOUR HEALING HOME

We have taken an amazing journey through your home together! I am so grateful to get to be there with you every step of the way. You have taken the reins in your life more than ever. You have owned your space and your life. You have claimed your home and optimized it with grace. I am so proud of you! Keep being present to your home and its energy and let the many helpers in your life ease your journey and light your way. You deserve to be happy, healthy, and at peace. Happy trails, and enjoy the beginning and end of each day, which starts and concludes in your beautiful healing home.

Yours in joy,

Amy

XO

ACKNOWLEDGMENTS

*H*op on to amyleighmercree.com/healinghomebookresources to get my digital guide to healthy living with the best sites to check your tap water and household products. Plus, get my resources and up-to-date information on many options for safer EMFs in the home, non-VOC products, and some of my favorite natural, nontoxic products for the home and body. You will also find printable resource lists for your feng shui and Vastu cures and my favorite chakra healing tools, plus printable aromatherapy recipes including nontoxic DIY Laundry Detergent. Plus get playlists of music for each chakra to balance the energy of your body and home.

I have been incredibly fortunate to be guided for over ten years by my extraordinary literary agent, Lisa Hagan. She is a truly kind and enlightened soul who happens to also be a cracker jack book agent. I am truly blessed to work with her.

It has been a continual windfall to work with my talented editor, Kate Zimmermann. She has been a tremendous partner in sharing this, and our nine other books, with the world. Life smiled upon me when I met her!

The talented team at Sterling has produced a gorgeous book, and I am so thrilled to work with them! Thank you, to the illustrator Nina Chakrabarti and Gina Bonanno for designing this beautiful book, and thank you, Blanca Oliviery, for helping to market this book with care and innovation. Also, tremendous thanks to the sales team, including sales representatives who sell the book across the country.

Karen Rauch Carter introduced me to how effective feng shui can be, and what an introduction it was! It was complete with falling ceiling fans, broken glass, a visit from some helpful police officers, and a spectacularly enhanced life. I am so grateful for all of her insight and knowledge.

My late medicine teacher, Laurie, shared massive knowledge and passed it on, along with the beautiful oral tradition passed down to her by her teacher and for many generations. I am so grateful to have had the time I did with her to receive a complete foundation for my work as a medical intuitive. Thank you, Laurie.

Annaliese Klein of Silver Wave Acupuncture has imparted an incredible amount of valuable knowledge, including increasing my depth of understanding of Taoism and Traditional Chinese Medicine. Not only has she enhanced my work as a medical intuitive, but she has also contributed to my deeper grasp of concepts applied to the home in this book. Thank you, Anna.

Sarah Hall of Sarah Hall Productions planted the seed for this book back in 2019, and here it is in book form! Thank you, Sarah, for your guidance and wisdom.

Thank you to my soul sister, Jenna, for joining our family and being so wonderful and a kickass girl-boss sister.

My medicine and soul sister, Jamie Eslinger, has been with me every step of the way: encouraging, analyzing, evolving, understanding, advising, supporting, and throwing bouquets of flowers out of the back of our proverbial convertible while speaking in silly accents. I don't know what I'd do without her. I also got an awesome brother from another mister and mother, Justin, out of the deal, so that's a double bonus.

I love my clients. They are my teachers! I'm so grateful for them and all of the beauty they bring to the world.

And you, dear reader, this is all for you. I am truly thankful for you. You are resplendent because you are reading this book and bettering yourself, your life, your home, and your world. You are radiant in your uniqueness. Keep shining.

REFERENCES

"A to Z Flowers | The Ultimate Flower Database." https://www.atozflowers.com/.

Abraham, Anna, and Paromita Chakraborty. 2020. "A Review on Sources and Health Impacts of Bisphenol A." *Reviews on Environmental Health* 35 (2): 201–10. https://doi.org/10.1515/reveh-2019-0034.

Alkafajy, Seeham Ali Qasim, and Rawaa Abdul-Ameer Abdul-Jabbar. 2020. "Comprehensive Effects of Parabens in Human Physiology." *Annals of Tropical Medicine and Public Health* 23 (20). https://doi.org/10.36295/asro.2020.232242.

Aron, Elaine N. 1997. *The Highly Sensitive Person: How to Thrive When the World Overwhelms You*. New York: Harmony Books.

Balcony Garden Web. 2019. "25 Best Houseplants for Kids." April 26, 2019. https://balconygardenweb.com/best-houseplants-for-kids/.

Bellieni, C. V., I. Pinto, A. Bogi, et al. 2012. "Exposure to Electromagnetic Fields from Laptop Use of 'Laptop' Computers." *Archives of Environmental & Occupational Health* 67 (1): 31–36. https://doi.org/10.1080/19338244.2011.564232.

Benjamin, Sailas, Eiji Masai, Naofumi Kamimura, et al. 2017. "Phthalates Impact Human Health: Epidemiological Evidences and Plausible Mechanism of Action." *Journal of Hazardous Materials* 340 (October): 360–83. https://doi.org/10.1016/j.jhazmat.2017.06.036.

Błędzka, Dorota, Jolanta Gromadzińska, and Wojciech Wąsowicz. 2014. "Parabens. From Environmental Studies to Human Health." *Environment International* 67 (June): 27–42. https://doi.org/10.1016/j.envint.2014.02.007.

Brown, Simon G. 2005. *The Feng Shui Bible: The Definitive Guide to Practising Feng Shui.* New York: Sterling Ethos.

Campanale, Claudia, Carmine Massarelli, Ilaria Savino, et al. 2020. "A Detailed Review Study on Potential Effects of Microplastics and Additives of Concern on Human Health." *International Journal of Environmental Research and Public Health* 17 (4): 1212. https://doi.org/10.3390/ijerph17041212.

Carter, Karen Rauch. 2000. *Move Your Stuff, Change Your Life: How to Use Feng Shui to Get Love, Money, Respect and Happiness.* New York: Simon and Schuster.

Cirino, Erica, and Karen Lamoreux. 2021. "Should You Be Worried About EMF Exposure?" *Healthline*, July 8, 2021. https://www.healthline.com/health/emf.

Clifford, Garth C. 2020. "Phoenix Symbolism & Meaning (+Totem, Spirit & Omens)." *World Birds* (blog). May 16, 2020. https://www.worldbirds.org/phoenix-symbolism/.

Cox, Kathleen M. 2000. *Vastu Living: Creating a Home for the Soul.* New York: Marlowe & Company.

DeBaun, Daniel T., and Ryan P. DeBaun. 2017. *Radiation Nation— Complete Guide to EMF Protection & Safety: The Proven Health Risks of Electromagnetic Radiation (EMF) & What to Do Protect Yourself & Family.* White River Junction, VT: Icaro Publishing.

Dutta, Sudipta, Diana K. Haggerty, Daniel A. Rappolee, et al. 2020. "Phthalate Exposure and Long-Term Epigenomic Consequences: A Review." *Frontiers in Genetics* 11 (May): 405. https://doi.org/10.3389/fgene.2020.00405.

Editors of Encyclopaedia Britannica. "Tara | Description & Facts." Encyclopedia Britannica. https://www.britannica.com/topic/Tara-Buddhist-goddess.

EM and RF Testing Solutions. "EMF & RF Testing | Mitigation | Shielding Experts." EM and RF Testing Solutions. Accessed May 18, 2021. http://www.emfrf.com/.

Gupta, Shiwangi, Radhey Shyam Sharma, and Rajeev Singh. 2020. "Non-Ionizing Radiation as Possible Carcinogen." *International Journal of Environmental Health Research*, September 2020: 1–25. https://doi.org/10.1080/09603123.2020.1806212.

Havas, Magda. 2017. "When Theory and Observation Collide: Can Non-Ionizing Radiation Cause Cancer?" *Environmental Pollution* 221 (February): 501–5. https://doi.org/10.1016/j.envpol.2016.10.018.

Hess, Katie. 2016. *Flowerevolution: Blooming into Your Full Potential with the Magic of Flowers*. Carlsbad, CA: Hay House.

"Introduction to VOCS and Health." Indoor Air Quality Scientific Findings Resource Bank (IAQ-SFRB). Accessed May 17, 2021. https://iaqscience.lbl.gov/.

Krishna, Talavane. 2001. *The Vaastu Workbook: Using the Subtle Energies of the Indian Art of Placement to Enhance Health, Prosperity, and Happiness in Your Home*. Rochester, VT: Destiny Books.

Lucey, Helen. 2020. "5 Tips for Safer Cell Phone Use During the Covid-19 Pandemic." Environmental Working Group (EWG). November 16, 2020. https://www.ewg.org/news-insights/news/5-tips-safer-cell-phone-use-during-covid-19-pandemic.

Melody. 1995. *Love Is in the Earth—A Kaleidoscope of Crystals Update: The Reference Book Describing the Metaphysical Properties of the Mineral Kingdom*. Edited by R. R. Jackson. Wheat Ridge, CO: Earth-Love Publishing House.

Mercola, Joseph. 2020. *EMF*D: 5G, Wi-Fi & Cell Phones: Hidden Harms and How to Protect Yourself (Illustrated Edition)*. Carlsbad, CA: Hay House.

Mercree, Amy Leigh. 2016. *The Chakras and Crystals Cookbook: Juices, Sorbets, Smoothies, Salads, and Soups to Empower Your Energy Centers*. New York: Allegria Entertainment.

———. 2018a. *Essential Oils Handbook: Recipes for Natural Living*. New York: Sterling Ethos.

———. 2018b. *A Little Bit of Mindfulness: An Introduction to Being Present*. Vol. 13. New York: Sterling Ethos.

———. 2019a. *A Little Bit of Goddess: An Introduction to the Divine Feminine*. Vol. 20. New York: Sterling Ethos.

———. 2019b. *The Mood Book: Crystals, Oils, and Rituals to Elevate Your Spirit*. New York: Sterling Ethos.

———. 2020. *A Little Bit of Meditation: An Introduction to Mindfulness*. Vol. 7. New York: Sterling Ethos.

Mercree, Chad, and Amy Leigh Mercree. 2016. *A Little Bit of Chakras: An Introduction to Energy Healing*. Vol. 5. New York: Sterling Ethos.

Mildon, Emma. 2018. *Evolution of Goddess: A Modern Girl's Guide to Activating Your Feminine Superpowers*. New York: Atria/Enliven Books.

Miller, Anthony B., Margaret E. Sears, L. Lloyd Morgan, et al. 2019. "Risks to Health and Well-Being from Radio-Frequency Radiation Emitted by Cell Phones and Other Wireless Devices." *Frontiers in Public Health* 7 (August): 223. https://doi.org/10.3389/fpubh.2019.00223.

Mortazavi, S.A.R., S. Taeb, S.M.J. Mortazavi, et al. 2016. "The Fundamental Reasons Why Laptop Computers Should Not Be Used on Your Lap." *Journal of Biomedical Physics & Engineering* 6 (4): 279–84.

Murphy-Hiscock, Arin. 2017. *The Green Witch: Your Complete Guide to the Natural Magic of Herbs, Flowers, Essential Oils, and More*. New York: Simon and Schuster.

Mustieles, Vicente, and Mariana F. Fernández. 2020. "Bisphenol A Shapes Children's Brain and Behavior: Towards an Integrated Neurotoxicity Assessment Including Human Data." *Environmental Health: A Global Access Science Source* 19 (1): 66. https://doi.org/10.1186/s12940-020-00620-y.

National Cancer Institute. 2019. "Electromagnetic Fields & Cancer." January 3, 2019. https://www.cancer.gov/about-cancer/causes-prevention/risk/radiation/electromagnetic-fields-fact-sheet.

National Institute of Environmental Health Sciences. "Electric & Magnetic Fields." U.S. Department of Health and Human Services. Accessed May 18, 2021. https://www.niehs.nih.gov/health/topics/agents/emf/index.cfm.

Peters, Amanda Gibby. 2019. *Simple Shui for Every Day: 365 Ways to Feng Shui Your Life*. Independently published.

Pineault, Nicolas. 2017. *The Non-Tinfoil Guide to EMFs: How to Fix Our Stupid Use of Technology*. CreateSpace Independent Publishing Platform.

Pitchford, Paul. 2002. *Healing with Whole Foods: Asian Traditions and Modern Nutrition*. Berkeley, CA: North Atlantic Books.

Reichstein, Gail. 1998. *Wood Becomes Water: Chinese Medicine in Everyday Life*. New York: Kodansha America.

Schumacher, Mark. 2013. "Protectors of Children, Goddesses of Motherhood, Patrons of Easy Delivery, Bringer of Children. Japanese Buddhism & Shintoism Photo Dictionary." On Mark Productions. 2013. https://www.onmarkproductions.com/html/child-protectors.html.

———. 2020. "Goddess Benzaiten, A-to-Z Dictionary of Japanese Buddhist / Shinto Statues." On Mark Productions. April 30, 2020. https://www.onmark-productions.com/html/benzaiten.shtml.

Singh, Z., and S. Bhalla. 2017. "Toxicity of Synthetic Fibres & Health." *Advance Research Inn Textile Engineering* 2 (1): 1012.

Stiles, K. G. 2020. *Chinese Medicine Guidebook: Essential Oils to Balance the Fire Element & Organ Meridians*. Draft2Digital.

Tade, Rahul S., Mahesh P. More, V. K. Chatap, et al. 2018. "Safety and Toxicity Assessment of Parabens in Pharmaceutical and Food Products." *Inventi Rapid: Pharmacy Practice* 3 (April): 1–9.

"Teaching Kids About Flowers and Their Meanings: 9 Great Examples."
2017. *Everything Backyard* (blog). January 24, 2017. https://everythingback-yard.net/kids-flowers-and-their-meanings/.

"The Most Intelligent Birds in the World." 2017. *Wingspan Optics*
(blog). September 1, 2017. https://wingspanoptics.com/blogs/field-journal/the-most-intelligent-birds-in-the-world.

"Traditional Tibetan Tingsha Cymbals | Meaning and Origins."Buddha
Groove. https://www.buddhagroove.com/buddhist-ritual-tool-tingsha/.

US Environmental Protection Agency. 2019. "What Are Volatile Organic
Compounds (VOCs)?" Overviews and Factsheets. August 1, 2019. https://www.epa.gov/indoor-air-quality-iaq/what-are-volatile-organic-compounds-vocs.

———. 2021. "Volatile Organic Compounds' Impact on Indoor Air Quality."
Overviews and Factsheets. February 10, 2021. https://www.epa.gov/indoor-air-quality-iaq/volatile-organic-compounds-impact-indoor-air-quality.

"Volatile Organic Compounds (VOCs) in Your Home." Minnesota
Department of Health. Accessed May 17, 2021. https://www.health.state.mn.us/communities/environment/air/toxins/voc.htm.

"What Are Phthalates? | Uses, Benefits, and Safety Facts." 2021. Chemical
Safety Facts. March 1, 2021. https://www.chemicalsafetyfacts.org/phthalates/.

Other Books by Amy Leigh Mercree

A Little Bit of Chakras: An Introduction to Energy Healing

The Chakras and Crystals Cookbook: Juices, Smoothies, Sorbets, Salads, and Crystal Infusions to Empower Your Energy Centers

A Little Bit of Meditation: An Introduction to Mindfulness

Recipes for Natural Living: Essential Oils Handbook

Recipes for Natural Living: Apple Cider Vinegar Handbook

A Little Bit of Mindfulness: An Introduction to Being Present

The Mood Book: Crystals, Oils, and Rituals to Elevate Your Spirit

A Little Bit of Goddess: An Introduction to the Divine Feminine

A Little Bit of Chakras: Your Personal Path to Energy Healing Guided Journal

A Little Bit of Meditation: Your Personal Path to Mindfulness Guided Journal

A Little Bit of Mindfulness: Your Personal Path to Awareness Guided Journal

100 Days to Calm: A Journal for Finding Everyday Tranquility

PICTURE CREDITS

All illustrations by Nina Chakrabarti, except the following:

Caroline M. Casey: 129, 144

Callie Hegstrom/Design Cuts: throughout (watercolor backgrounds)

iStock/Getty Images Plus: Dksamco: xxii; Anastasiia Kurman: 6 (apple)

Kennedy Liggett: xxv, xxix

Briit Sabo: xxiii

Alexis Seabrook: 161

Shutterstock.com: a_ptichkina: 65; airdynamic: 169; Amber_Sun: 101; Analgin: 6 (flower); Ardea-studio: 15, endpaper; arxichtu4ki: 75; Asolo: 43; Atomorfen Illustration: 117; Julia August: 143 (garland); Barv_Art: 100; Bidadash: 115; cat_arch_angel: 112; Dinkoobraz: xxxii; Dneprstock: 154; Elinwool: 27, 41 (lamp); enra: 160, 161, 164; Elena Eskevich: xiv; Flash Vector: 126; Peter Hermes Furian: 16; GL Sonts: xxx; Maria Goltsova: 141; Gulman Anya: 53; Jenny Klein: 143 (shell group); Kochkanyan Juliya: 123; ladyfortune: 145; Le Panda: 62, 148; Macrovector: xix, 25; Maltiase: xvi; Elena Medvedeva: 28; mimibubu: 41 (nightstand); Maria Minina: 14; Mona Monash: 122; olgers: 143 (shell); patrimonio designs ltd: 166 (green man); piixypeach: v; Elena Pimonova: 130; Popkova: 116; P.S.Art-Design-Studio: 145; Elizaveta Ruzanova: 54; samui: 17; Ekaterina Shagaeva: 156, 158; Sidhe: xxviii; Alena Solonshchikova: 5, 23, 31, 36, 63, 71, 76, 86, 113, 118, 134; Sunnydream: 55; Supawadee: 21; svetalik: 46; Tarina_neko: 32; Daria Ustiugova: 34, 78, 138; watercolor 15: throughout (watercolor); Lena Yevsikova: 166 (tools); Phoebe Yu: 85; Yurumi: 142; Lyubov Zaytseva: 33; Katya Zlobina: 47

INDEX

Notes

NOTES

 NOTES

NOTES

NOTES

NOTES

NOTES

Notes

About the Author

*A*my Leigh Mercree is an internationally acclaimed medical intuitive with over twenty years of experience. She specializes in spirit guides with a focus on shamanism, healing your home, and holistic wellness. Using a combination of spirituality and science, Amy's job is finding the root cause of imbalances in the body. Clients come to her with health issues that they have not had results healing elsewhere, and Amy helps them to get to the absolute root cause of the problem and put together a plan for how to fix it. She's helped thousands of people find the root causes of numerous mild and moderate medical conditions and uncover their bodies' wisdom to heal permanently.

Amy is a best-selling author of fifteen books, a media personality, a holistic health expert, and a mystic teacher. She instructs internationally, sharing Meet Your Goddess Guides, Ancestral and Karmic Shamanism, and The Healing Home Masterclass.

Mercree has been featured in *Glamour Magazine*, *Women's Health*, *Inc.*, *Shape*, *Huffington Post*, *Your Tango*, *Soul and Spirit*, *MindBodyGreen*, CBS, NBC, Hello Giggles, *Reader's Digest*, *O, The Oprah Magazine*, *Forbes*, ABC, *First for Women*, *Country Living*, CW, FOX, *Bustle*, *Well+Good*, *Refinery29*, Hello Glow, SheKnows, Thrive Global, *Spartan*, *Poosh*, *Parade*, Oprah Daily, and many more.

Mercree is the author of *The Spiritual Girl's Guide to Dating,* *Joyful Living, The Compassion Revolution, A Little Bit of Chakras, The Chakras and Crystals Cookbook, A Little Bit of Meditation, Recipes for Natural Living: Essential Oils Handbook, Recipes for Natural Living: Apple Cider Vinegar Handbook, A Little Bit of Mindfulness, The Mood Book, A Little Bit of Goddess, A Little Bit of Chakras Guided Journal, A Little Bit of Meditation Guided Journal, A Little Bit of Mindfulness Guided Journa*l, and *100 Days to Calm.*

If you'd like to learn more, join The Healing Home Masterclass to learn *all* the tricks of the trade and learn how to talk to your spirit guides to elevate your home and life. Connect with Amy at amyleighmercree.com and @AmyLeighMercree on Instagram, Facebook, Pinterest, and get a boatload of free bonus content at amyleighmercree.com/healinghomebookresources.

Tag Amy on your favorite social platform and share your #thehealinghome pictures! She will repost you and can't wait to see your progress.